SO, YOU'RE RAISING YOUR GRANDKIDS!

TESTED TIPS, RESEARCH, & REAL-LIFE STORIES TO MAKE YOUR LIFE EASIER

HARRIET HODGSON

Virginia

Published in the United States by WriteLife Publishing
(An imprint of Boutique of Quality Books Publishing Company)
www.writelife.com

978-1-60808-189-9 (p)
978-1-60808-190-5 (e)

LCCN: 2018932507

Book design by Robin Krauss, www.bookformatters.com
Cover photo from istockphotos.com
Cover design by Marla Thompson, www.edgeofwater.com
Interior photos by Haley Earley, Independent Photographer

First editor: Michelle Booth

Second editor: Olivia Swenson

Praise for *So, You're Raising Your Grandkids!*

Very, Very Complete

So, You're Raising Your Grandkids! is well written and very, very complete. There are many practical tips on how to have a good life as a grandparent parenting again. The stories, the suggestions, the personal stories are all here. This is a guide from someone who has walked the walk!

—Beverly Sullivan,
former Grandparent Raising Grandchildren

A Gift for All GRGs

Out of great tragedy and loss has come this inspiring, practical book—a gift for all GRGs. *So, You're Raising Your Grandkids!* is like a wise friend, able to be honest about the challenges of being a GRG, while being positive about the rewards. Eight well-organized chapters combine practical advice and wisdom from Harriet's GRG experience. The superb, extensive research, coupled with insightful stories, contribute to a most helpful book. Harriet's example gives us hope that strength will be there when we need it. Her focus is on kindness and love, and she believes love can lead us and take us where we need to go.

—Judith Seward, MS,
Grandparent Raising Grandchildren

An Indispensable Guide

To describe Harriet Hodgson as an expert in caregiving would be an understatement. For more than two decades, she's found herself in the role of caregiver with three generations of family members, including her mother, her twin grandchildren, and now her husband. Through it all, she's managed to maintain her career as a health and wellness journalist, the author of 36 books, and a popular public speaker. In this information-packed guide, she enhances the sound and practical advice found in *Help, I'm Raising My Grandkids*, adding research and family stories that illustrate her points and demonstrate her hard-won wisdom. Readers will appreciate her frank discussion of some of the sacrifices and compromises that come with raising grandchildren, along with her helpful suggestions for coping. For grandparents who unexpectedly find themselves in a parenting role, this book is an indispensable and most welcome guide.

—Marty Tousley, RNM, MS, FT, DCC, Grief Counselor,
Moderator of Grief Discussion Groups

Should Be Required Reading

This book is so thorough I feel it should be required reading for university students who are pursuing caregiving professions: teachers, counselors, therapists, and doctors.

—Thomas Brandy,
Retired Teacher and Behavioral Counselor

Provides Hope and Support

So, You're Raising Your Grandkids! is a must read for any grandparents who are currently raising their grandchildren or are functioning as parents to their grandchildren. Harriet Hodgson has crafted a book that is conversational, easy to read, and contains great practical tools and valuable resources. Harriet also covers in detail the challenges presented to grandparents who experience both loss due to death and symbolic loss, both of which are prominent in the grandparent's world. Perhaps, the greatest asset of Harriet's latest work is her transparency about her experiences raising her grandchildren, which provides both hope and support for those grandparents in similar circumstances.

—Dave Roberts, LMSW,
Adjunct Professor of Psychology, Utica College,
HuffPost Contributor, parent who has
experienced the death of a child

Revealing and Uplifting

Harriet has assembled an awesome book and guide! Based on her own life experiences, extensive research, and conversations with people all over the country, this book is a lifeline for a segment of the population that few realize is so extensive. Almost everyone knows one or more retirees that are raising their grandkids—some are raising their great-grandkids. Harriet's personal stories are revealing and uplifting, showing there is help for anyone providing care for children. She covers so many important topics and buttresses them with excellent research. Caring for the emotional needs of the children who have suffered a personal trauma, dealing with extended family that are not always supportive, dealing with school teachers and administration, and more—her advice is ultimately practical. The bibliography, list of websites, and other items in the appendix are a great source of additional information.

—Mark Schultz

Recommended for All Grandparents

This book about parenting grandchildren is very thorough and informative. It is filled with practical suggestions and is well–illustrated by Harriet's experiences. Information from many other relevant sources is useful. The chapter on grieving would be especially helpful to both grandparents and grandchildren. I recommend this book to all grandparents!

—Joanne Mair, RN, MS,
Retired Nurse Educator, grandmother of nine

Whatever the reason you now find yourself a GRG, Harriet's beautifully written, well-researched, personal, and sensitive book will help guide you through the many adjustments you have to make as a grandparent faced with parenting again. Harriet has filled this book with her own heartfelt stories and compiled resources and support to help you get through your own experience. She helps us focus on the joys of seeing the world through young eyes again---a gift for all caregivers.

—Adrienne Gruberg, President and Founder
The Caregiver Space

Other Books by Harriet Hodgson
from WriteLife Publishing

The Family Caregiver's Guide: How to Care for a Loved One at Home

Affirmations for Family Caregivers

A Journal for Family Caregivers: A Place for Thoughts, Plans, and Dreams

The Family Caregiver's Cookbook: Easy-Fix Recipes for Busy Family Caregivers

Happy Again! Your New and Meaningful Life after Loss

For more information about Harriet Hodgson's books please visit www.writelife.com and www.harriethodgson.com

This book is dedicated to my daughter,
Helen Anne Hodgson Welby, mother of my twin grandchildren.
You are in my heart and always will be.

Contents

Foreword

Let me begin with open disclosure. I am a grandparent. I have two grandchildren. Kenny, age eight years old at this writing, and Lucy, now five years old. I was deeply honored when my son, Michael, and his wife, Angelina, named their first child after me. Both children are a joy to me. I live close to them and do all the grandparenting things—taking them to school on days that I am home, babysitting on a moment's notice, helping with homework, buying gifts, and watching their games and competitions.

Research has supported the important role of grandparents. Grandparents can be a critical resource to the child and parent, offering time, talent, and treasure to their grandchild. They can receive much as well—a sense of biological and familial continuity, the stimulation of being with a young child, seeing the world anew through that child's eyes, and the sense of vicarious achievement in the small and large accomplishments of the grandchild.

Like many grandparents, I enjoy the role. And like many grandparents, I especially enjoy the limited and privileged involvement often identified with the role. A brief anecdote may describe it. When Kenny was three years old, he was in the backseat of my car as we picked up pizza for a family supper. I noticed Kenny nervously looking out the back window, and asked him what was wrong.

Kenny warned, "You have to be careful, Grandpa. The moon can follow you home." I was fascinated with the response and Kenny then taught me all about space. The stars, it seems, are very far up and you need one, maybe two, big ladders to reach them. You have to be careful though; they are hot like light bulbs. After Kenny went to sleep, I recounted the story to my son and daughter-in-law. My son laughed and reminded me that he would have received a lecture on astronomy. He was right.

We often teach our children but learn from our grandchildren. It is a very different relationship. Like the old saw says, we spoil them and give them back to their parents. And quite frankly, as much as I enjoy them, I also enjoy, after a day, giving them back. In my my sixties, they can exhaust me.

What happens, though, when you cannot give them back? What happens when situations such as divorce, death, or economic upheaval create a situation where grandparents have to raise their grandchildren? Almost one out of ten grandparents has this role, either raising or having a significant role in raising a grandchild. Such a situation is wrought with complications.

First, grandparents raising grandchildren inevitably results from some form of loss—a child dies, divorces, loses a job, falls to addiction, or has physical or mental health difficulties. So grandparents must not only deal with their own disappointments and grief, but also the grief of the grandchildren. They are truly wounded healers. One of the things I like most about Hodgson's book is that she acknowledges this grief.

Second, the reality is that as one ages, it is difficult to cope with the boundless energy of a child, the inherent drama of an adolescent, and the unceasing demands of parenthood. It is exhausting. Moreover, at a time when sources of income may be more limited, the expenses of raising a child can be daunting.

Third, one's sense of an assumptive world is challenged. This is not the way it [life] is supposed to be. Both grandparent and grandchild have to deal with the constant incongruity inherent in this context. That too, is a source of grief. This grief is often disenfranchised—that is, unacknowledged by others, perhaps even one's self. It is difficult, outside of a support group, to really explore the inherent ambivalence of such a role. It is equally difficult to be pitied for raising grandchildren, or unrealistically portrayed as a saint, when all you are doing is coping with the hand you were dealt.

Happily, Harriet Hodgson's book *So, You're Raising Your Grandkids!* is a most useful resource to grandparents in that role and those who seek to understand and assist them. Hodgson offers not only critical validation, but practical suggestions to navigate this difficult terrain. Hodgson writes from her experience. In her seventies, the sudden deaths of her daughter and former son-in-law brought her fifteen-year-old grandchildren to her door. In some ways, her situation may be considered atypical. Hodgson had resources to draw upon as both she and her husband were educated professionals, happily married, and reasonably prosperous. The twins, though dealing with sudden loss, seemed stable and well-adjusted. Yet they were still thrown into the tumult of a life suddenly changed. In recounting her struggles, Hodgson offers counsel that transcends any differences of class, ethnicity, or circumstances. Not only are Hodgson's story and advice useful, she has also packed the book with additional resources, such as organizations and Internet support for grandparents now thrust into a parenting role.

Raising grandchildren is challenging even in the best of situations and circumstances. Yet Hodgson's book makes it a little less lonely, offering critical reassurance, even when one does not have the freedom to give children back to their parents.

—Kenneth J. Doka, PhD, Professor, Graduate School, College of New Rochelle, and Senior Consultant, the Hospice Foundation of America

Introduction

When the phone rang I was just drifting off to sleep. The jarring sound awakened me instantly. Who would be calling at this hour?

"Hello," I answered tentatively.

"There's been an accident," the caller said. "Your granddaughter was injured and taken to the hospital by ambulance. Your daughter was injured and taken to the hospital by helicopter. Her injuries are really bad."

I shared this news with my husband, John, in a surprisingly calm voice. We dressed quickly and drove to the hospital emergency department. Our granddaughter had a mild concussion and our daughter was in surgery. As the hours passed, more surgeons were called in to assist. The lead surgeon came out to talk with us. He said the medical team would fix one problem and another would appear. Twenty hours later we received the news we had been dreading. Our daughter was brain-dead.

John and I signed legal documents to cease medical support and signed additional documents to donate her organs. Then we went into surgery to say good-bye. Our granddaughter, who had been dismissed from the emergency room, came with us, along with our grandson. They were fifteen-year-old fraternal twins and our only grandchildren. Blunt force trauma had caused our daughter's face to swell, and she didn't look like herself. The twins stood beside the gurney, looked at their mother, and sobbed uncontrollably. I wondered if they would survive such tragedy. Would I?

Helen's death not only robbed us of a daughter, it robbed us of a future with her. At that moment, I had no idea there was more tragedy to come. Two days later, on the same weekend, my father-in-law (Pampa) succumbed to pneumonia. Although I had been anticipating his death for months, it still came as a shock. Pampa was the patriarch of the family, and we would miss his exuberant personality and laughter. We would also miss his wisdom.

Our former son-in-law offered to move into the house with the twins and live with them until they graduated from high school. Since we were in our seventies and reeling from shock, we accepted his offer. His kindness enabled us to rest and regroup. Unfortunately, my grief didn't subside with time; it became worse. Eight weeks after Pampa's death my brother, and only sibling, died of a heart attack. He had just finished a course of treatment for cancer. Apparently, he survived the treatment, but his heart did not. In the fall of the same year, the twins' father died from the injuries he received in another car crash.

I couldn't believe it. Sometimes I still can't believe it.

Four deaths in a row were too much, and I turned to my family for help. The members of my extended family became a support group. Friends, books, articles, and grief organizations were other sources of help. To my surprise, I used my bachelor of science degree in early childhood education from Wheelock College. Putting the child first is the focus of Wheelock College, and I kept this focus in mind as I raised my grandkids. Breaking down information into smaller parts, another benefit of my college courses, also came in handy. If you had told me I would be using my degree at this stage of life, I would have said you were delusional. But I used this training time and again. I wish I could have afforded a full-page newspaper ad to thank Wheelock, but I couldn't, so I thank the college here. Wheelock College shaped my life and shaped the twins' lives.

Relatives thought I should write a book about raising our

grandchildren. "Do it for the family," my brother-in-law advised. Though I thought about the idea, I didn't act on it because of the challenges it presented, with confidentiality at the top of the list. I didn't want to hurt the twins in any way. Rabbi Earl Grollman changed my mind. He had written a mini review for the cover of my previous book and liked the book so much he called me.

"You're a good writer," he said. "You should write about raising your grandchildren."

My feelings swung back and forth like a pendulum. Yes, I'll write it. No, I won't. Yes, I'll write it. No, I won't. I thought about Rabbi Grollman's suggestion for weeks and finally figured out how to do it. I would tell my personal story, weave research findings into it, and add practical tips from experience. I'm profoundly grateful to Rabbi Grollman for his encouragement and kindness. And I'm profoundly grateful to Kenneth J. Doka, PhD, for his insightful foreword. Dr. Doka's story about his grandson, Kenny, is charming, childlike, and makes me smile.

You may be looking for help if you're raising a grandchild now, or about to begin the journey. Well, help has arrived. What does this book have for you? It is written in an easy-to-read style and contains practical tips that can get you from one hour to the next, one day to the next, and one week to the next. If you're desperate, turn to the "What Works" lists at the end of the chapters. These lists summarize key tips in each chapter. For quick reference, the tips are printed in bold.

This book is based on my extensive caregiving experience and research. The first version of this book was published in 2012 and written in the present tense. I didn't have time to spread the word about it, however, because my husband's aorta dissected in 2013. He had three emergency operations and, during the third one, suffered a spinal cord injury that paralyzed his legs. Looking back now, I realize I became John's caregiver the night I drove him to the hospital. The twins are grown now, living their own lives, and pursuing their own dreams. Therefore, this version is written in the past tense.

At first, I thought I was revising a book I had previously written. As I added new research, new chapters on grief and grandparents' sacrifices, additional family stories, and updates on my grandchildren, the book evolved into something different. This is a new book, and comes from my twenty-one years of caregiving experience. I've cared for three generations of family members. My mother had vascular dementia, and I was her family caregiver for nine years. John and I cared for the twins for seven years. I've been John's caregiver for five years, with more years to come.

You may feel alone at this time of life, but you aren't. According to the 2010 US Government Census, 4.9 million children are being raised by their grandparents. This number is undoubtedly higher now. Two acronyms have come from the trend: GRG for grandparents raising grandchildren, and GAP for grandparents as parents. Recent literature includes a new term, *grandparent carer*, which is hard to say, but descriptive. Like all grandparents in the caregiving trenches, some days will go well, and other days won't. This is normal. You've joined a club, the Grandparents Raising Grandchildren Club, and it's one of the best in the world.

I want you to feel like you're sitting at the kitchen table, chatting with me and getting to know each other. If we were really doing this, we might laugh together, tell a few jokes, and hug each other. You and I are linked by our mission—to protect, care for, encourage, and love our grandchildren more each day. What a blessing!

Harriet Hodgson

CHAPTER 1

The Growing GRG Trend

Grandparents raising grandchildren (GRG) is a growing trend. As the trend spread across the country, state governments developed resources to help GRGs and GAPs, including support groups, booklets, pamphlets, conferences, and blogs. Many grandparents are raising grandchildren because their own children got into trouble, something that's hard to admit. The fact that your child lost her or his way is a source of emotional pain. Each day, you ask yourself, "How did I get here?" This is a valid question and the answer is complicated.

How Did You Get Here?

Becoming a GRG can be an instant change, as it was for me, or a gradual one. In the back of your mind, you may have suspected that you would need to assume this role someday. You just didn't know this day would come so soon. While I was standing outside the hospital emergency department, the realization that I was going to be a GRG hit me like a lightning bolt. Without any warning, my life changed forever.

As a parent, you may have witnessed your child involved in risky behaviors, drug experimentation, drug/alcohol addiction, sexual activity, sexual promiscuity, petty theft, and/or running with the wrong crowd. Time and again, you tried to help, and nothing worked. Every morning you awakened with the hope that your child would choose a better path. That day never came. Things couldn't go on this way, so you made a difficult, life-altering decision, not knowing all it entailed, but knowing you would stick to it.

The Commitment to Care for Your Grandchild

This commitment came from love, and you vowed to honor it. Whatever it took, you would be at your grandchild's side—a shield, teacher, hugger, role model, and loving grandparent. Making this decision could have taken years, and you may wish you had made it sooner. Just as fog lifts in early morning, the fog cleared from your mind, and you saw life clearly. You dusted off your parenting instincts and stepped forward, even though the road would be long, the burden would be heavy, and the challenges would be great.

A *Chicago Tribune* article, "Grandparents Raising Grand-children," describes the shock Sandra and Terry Eck felt when their son called and asked his parents to care for his twenty-two-month-old son. "Of course we said yes," Sandra is quoted as saying. "The alternative was foster care." Agreeing to raise their grandchild turned the grandparents' lives upside down. They were in total shock, according to Sandra, and had to start life anew with a baby. Despite the challenges they faced, the Ecks are convinced they made the right decision.

You made the right decision and so did we. John and I felt we had to take action because the welfare of our grandchildren was at stake.

Driving home from a Girl Scout meeting on a snowy February

night, Helen turned from a rural road onto a main highway. Although she checked for oncoming traffic, she didn't see the car that hit her car broadside. The last thing Helen did in her life was to pat her daughter's leg to comfort her. Our grandchildren had terrible memories to process.

The days ahead were bleak for John and me: buy a burial plot, order a headstone, plan a memorial service, and help get the twins settled.

We had been part of their lives since the twins were born. We loved them dearly and had many fond memories of them. When they were infants, the twins wouldn't go to sleep unless they were facing each other. At their first birthday party, for some reason I imitated a chicken by flapping my elbows and making clucking sounds. The twins giggled, so I did the chicken imitation again. When I repeated the imitation a third time, a long, low laugh came from my grandson's mouth, and he gave me a look that implied, "You're a silly grandma."

As the twins grew, we babysat them often. We hung a swing from the back deck, and John built a seesaw for them. I stocked the family room cupboard with age-appropriate toys and games. After Helen and her husband divorced, we helped the family move several times. Ready and willing as we were to care for fifteen-year-olds, John and I had our doubts about the future.

We didn't tell the twins about our doubts because nothing would be gained by our admission. When we were alone, however, and had a chance to talk, we wondered if we had enough energy for the job. How would it feel to go through the teen years again? Had teens changed a lot since we raised our daughters? The worst thought, the one we were reluctant to speak aloud, was "What if we fail?" We could only try and do our best.

A list-maker since childhood, I made a list of the strengths I had to bring to the job, starting with my degree in child development.

I had raised teens before and could draw upon this experience. I had written articles about teens, and this research would come in handy. John and I were devoted to each other and had a calm and loving home, something the twins needed. I had many experiences to draw upon, and, thanks to birthdays, the wisdom that comes with age. Finally, I was determined to succeed.

One of my mottos is "Never mess with a determined grandma."

John had his own strengths to bring to his role. He was an experienced physician, a retired air force colonel, had traveled to many countries, volunteered with the Boy Scouts, was an outdoorsman, served on many committees, and had been secretary and president of an international organization. The people who worked with him thought John was one of the kindest people they had ever met. "I love your husband!" a nurse exclaimed. I told her I loved him too. Surely his experiences and a kind nature would help John with raising the twins.

Our family story spread around town quickly. We started to receive compliments and didn't know how to respond to them. One person thought raising grandkids assured us of a seat in heaven. A dear friend told us we were saints by the standards of any religion. Another friend explained, "When God closes a door, He opens a window." This comment confused us, but we knew she meant well. We also knew we were strong people, bereaved parents, and loving grandparents. Tragedy wasn't going to win, John and I decided. Life was going to win, and we would do everything we could to make this happen.

We knew people were trying to encourage us. Still, replying to their comments was difficult. We didn't know what to say. I narrowed my responses down to three: "Thank you," "Thank you for thinking of us," and "Please keep us in your thoughts." As our story spread further, friends and strangers felt compelled to share their sad stories with me. I had plenty of sad stories of my own and didn't need any more. To avoid a long conversation, I would look at my watch and announce, "Sorry, I have to run. I have a doctor's appointment." Although I felt bad about lying, I knew more sad stories would be emotionally harmful.

GRG is a growing team that spans all geographic, ethnic, and socio-economic boundaries. You're on the team. Even if your team has only one member, it's a team, and you're making a difference in a child's life. You have so much to give. You're providing shelter, food, and clothing on your own or with some help. You're providing the structure your grandchild needs. Most importantly, you're giving unconditional love to a vulnerable child. This foundation will serve your grandchild today and for many tomorrows.

Reasons for the Trend

Why are more grandparents raising their grandkids? The American Academy of Child and Adolescent Psychiatry lists the reasons for this national trend in its article, "Grandparents Raising Grandchildren." The reasons are what you might expect. Many reasons are painful and some may apply to the parent or parents of your grandchild. Other reasons are due to societal changes. Here are the reasons cited by the academy:

- More single-parent families
- High divorce rate
- Teen pregnancy
- Acquired Immune Deficiency Syndrome (AIDS)
- Parent or parents in jail
- Drug addiction

- Parental abuse and neglect

- Disability or death of parents

Expert after expert cites divorce as a major reason for the trend. Today, many couples take marriage lightly and, if it doesn't turn out as anticipated, divorce is the answer. If your adult child's divorce is pending, or if the divorce has been finalized, the best thing you can do for your grandchild is to stay out of the way. Avoid family squabbles because they will only make things worse. Tempted as you may be, don't get involved in the emotional crossfire.

K. R. Tremblay and colleagues write about the divorce issue in their article "Grandparents: As Parents," posted on the Colorado State University Extension website. They tell parents to be as amicable as possible and not take sides. Grandparents shouldn't let themselves be used as divorce weapons. Any attempts to do this need to be resisted and dealt with openly.

After Helen divorced we continued to treat the twins' father courteously. This was best for him, best for the twins, and best for us. We also wanted to model civil behavior. John and I never said anything against the twins' father. Of course, we discussed issues with our daughter, but these discussions were held when the twins weren't present. There's a big difference between keeping children informed and burdening them with information they aren't mature enough to understand. The twins' lives were already complicated, and they didn't need more complications from us.

After their mother died, the twins undoubtedly discussed their parents' divorce. Their bedrooms were upstairs, near each other, with a shared bathroom in between. This floor plan gave the twins many chances to talk. John and I could hear mumbling from upstairs, but couldn't discern any words. Neither of the twins brought up the topic of divorce with us. However, I think they discussed it with relatives. We didn't pry and figured if the twins wanted to talk with us, they would. One thing we knew for certain—divorce sends shock waves through the entire family.

Other reasons for the trend come from the US Department of Health and Human Services. In its article "Healthy Aging: Raising Children Again," the department cites mental illness, poverty, domestic violence, and military deployment as reasons why more grandparents have become responsible for raising their grandchildren. A deployed military parent may not know when she or he will return. You may be raising your grandchild because your adult child failed to be a responsible parent. An immature parent may suddenly realize that child-rearing is lots of work and abandon their child. A single parent may have a debilitating disease, such as multiple sclerosis.

Of all of these reasons, drug addiction is the prevailing reason for the trend according to a PBS News Hour story "How Drug Addiction Led to More Grandparents Raising Grandchildren." Opioid addiction is the main culprit, and the article compares it to the drug epidemics of the 1980s and 1990s. An addicted parent can't care for herself or himself or a child. Sadly, opioid addiction seems to be spreading. Television and print media seem to air an opioid addiction story every day. In fact, opioid addiction is a major public health problem in the US.

The sagging US economy also contributed to the trend. "The Granny Nanny Phenomenon," an article on the American Association of Retired Persons (AARP) website, reports that grandparents raising grandchildren face financial, health, education, and work challenges. These challenges can ruin retirement plans. The dream of going to Paris, France, for two weeks is gone in a flash. Updating your home, buying a new car, whatever your dream may be, is gone. The anonymous article says 20 percent of grandfamilies live in poverty. Lack of funds casts a pall on every aspect of life—food, shelter, clothing, nutrition, transportation, recreation, and future plans.

I think the worst reason for the trend is the death of a child. As a bereaved parent, I feel like part of my soul is missing. I will always be a bereaved parent and nothing can change this. There is no such thing as closure. Other bereaved parents feel the same way. Eventually, we learn to adjust to our losses and create new lives. But we still grieve. Most of our sobs are silent, yet we feel them in our gut. Sometimes, without any warning, we burst into tears.

While you're raising a grandchild, you must deal with your own feelings. You may feel ambivalent about becoming a GRG or GAP. The dictionary defines ambivalence as uncertainty or fluctuation, especially when caused by the inability to make a choice, or by a simultaneous desire to say or do two opposite things. Opposing feelings, such as love for your grandchildren and anger at your difficult child, are hard to process. Dueling feelings like these can linger for years. While you're feeling your feelings, you're also making adjustments for your grandchild. You may have given up a spare bedroom, for example, or a closet that you needed.

Whatever the reasons may be, the thought of raising a grandchild can make you gulp.

A Daunting Role

The twins were fifteen and a half years old when their mother died, and fifteen and three quarters when their father died. Every age is a terrible age to lose a parent. The teen years are especially hard because this is a time of exploration, probing, and self-discovery. John and I faced a huge challenge. Somehow, and we weren't sure how, we had to stay upbeat for the twins while grieving for four family members—our daughter, John's father, my brother, and the twins' father. You may be facing a daunting challenge now: increased property taxes, fewer work hours, or the diagnosis of a chronic illness. How should you proceed?

The only solution I can suggest is to focus on love. Give yourself credit for coming to the aid of a hurting child. The love you feel for your grandchild, and your grandchild's love for you, can keep you going short-term, and in the years to come.

We were fortunate grandparents, for when our twin grandchildren moved in with us they understood our family values of hard work, kindness, education, and setting goals. They also had good manners. Overcome with grief as they were, each of them thanked me for dinner when they left the table. Their thanks made me want to cry. Some grandparents aren't as fortunate as us and are caring for emotionally disturbed children. These GRGs try to adjust to the present and gird themselves for the future.

As the Academy of Child and Adolescent Psychiatry explains in the website article "Grandparents Raising Grandchildren," many children who are living with grandparents have psychological problems. Psychiatrists and psychologists call these "preexisting conditions" and they include physical abuse, emotional abuse, neglect, prenatal exposure to drugs and alcohol, and the loss of a parent due to death or imprisonment. Every condition is difficult for grandparents to handle. From the onset, raising a grandchild can become a waiting game, as grandparents ask, "What will happen next?"

The American Association for Marriage and Family Therapy, in the website article "Grandparents Raising Grandchildren" (the same title as several other articles), notes that children being raised by grandparents often have developmental, physical, behavioral, and emotional problems. A grandchild may have anxiety issues, learning disabilities, or aggressive behaviors. Perhaps you're caring for a baby who is learning to talk but doesn't have the vocabulary to express feelings. Yet the baby's behavior tells you something is wrong. In a case like this, it may be wise to consult a pediatrician.

From my child development training, I know babies show they're upset with general fussiness, crying more than usual, and banging their heads on their cribs. Toddlers who were making progress with toilet training may regress and start wetting again. Nursery school and kindergarten kids may return to thumb-sucking. While teenagers have extensive verbal skills, they may keep their feelings hidden. Instead of talking to you, a teenage grandchild may seek comfort from peers.

Jim Fay and Foster W. Cline, MD, authors of *Grandparenting With Love & Logic*, describe grandparenting as a straightforward job. Most of the time it is, but the grandparenting journey can be a winding road with turns, obstacles, and detours. GRGs and GAPs have a common dilemma—balancing protection and freedom. This is a push-pull situation. You push as you gently nudge your grandchild toward the future and adulthood. You pull when you bring your grandchild back to safety.

The push-pull response isn't a one-time thing. Rather, it is a continuous response that happens again and again as your grandchild matures. This response depends on your grandchild's age, emotional maturity, personality, experience, peer group, and environment. The push-pull scale is always in flux. You will have times when you barely push, and times when you pull back strongly.

Sure, it would be wonderful if raising a grandchild went smoothly all the time and there were no differences of opinion. That's not reality. You will probably have some family disagreements. Your grandchild's parents may oppose you at every turn. Are you going to buy into this behavior? Parents and grandparents need to pick their battles, according to Christina Frank, author of the article "The Need for Parenting Consistency." Frank has some simple advice for parents (and grandparents) and it is to "make rules . . . and bend some of them." I laughed when I read this because John and I did just that.

Family rules need to have some flexibility. Your grandchild may object to your rules in public and be secretly grateful for them in private. Maybe your grandchild doesn't want to go to a movie with friends because it received poor reviews. Why spend money on a lousy movie? Your grandchild can use you as an excuse. Having rules doesn't guarantee that every day will go well. Some days can be downright hard. If you're observant, however, and slow down to savor the moment, you will find joy in every day. Think about the laughter you've shared with your grandchild. And think about how you have changed.

Guilt, a Monster in the Room

Every grandparent wants the best for their grandchild. No matter how hard you work, chances are you'll find something to feel guilty about—lack of time, a blah dinner, losing your patience. Discouragement can take over and make you feel like you're doing a poor job, which increases guilt. I wish I could have shielded the twins from emotional pain. Since I was unable to do this, I felt guilty. I shared this thought with my brother-in-law. "You shouldn't feel guilty for something you couldn't control," he replied. He has a point.

Guilt can lead to poor decisions, such as lavishing toys on a grandchild to compensate for the lack of a parent or parents. Worse, guilt can sap joy from your day and become a monster in the room. You may be one of those grandparents who feels guilty about saying no. I think the failure to say no is a disservice to any grandchild because they will hear this word often in life. "No" helps a grandchild learn about personal safety and boundaries. From the moment the twins moved in with us, we expected them to eat dinner with us. That was the rule. Period. The twins weren't thrilled with this rule, but we stuck to it. We knew that children who ate dinner as a family did better in school and in life.

After the twins turned seventeen and had their driver's licenses, we eased up on some rules. Sometimes they went out for dinner with friends, but they ate most meals with us. As time passed, they looked forward to family dinners and would ask me what was on the menu.

Maybe you don't like the word *guilt* and prefer *regret* instead. Guilt can be a form of regret, a wish to turn back the clock, a chance to slip into "If only I had . . ." thinking. Before you know it, regret is out of control. Rabbi Earl A. Grollman writes about regret in his book *Straight Talk about Death for Teenagers*. "Blaming yourself and others won't bring him or her back to life," Grollman points out. Your guilt won't make up for a child's poor choices, incarceration, or military deployment, so you may as well move on. Don't let guilt drag you down.

Self-blame is another form of guilt. You can get stuck in self-blame for years. I think guilt takes up too much space in our minds and robs us of happiness. Guilt is usually a non-productive emotion (there are exceptions), and it's best to get rid of it. The question is, how? Start by gathering the facts, living mindfully, asking for help, staying socially connected, and practicing self-care. You need to take care of yourself in order to care for your grandchild. Keep in mind that your grandchild may also feel guilty for what has transpired.

A young child may feel guilty about not being good enough. An abusive parent may use guilt to retain control. You're in charge now and can tell your grandchild that she or he is safe and worthy of love. Older kids may notice you running around, working really hard, and feel guilty about causing extra work. Once, when I was kidding my granddaughter, I said she probably thought I was stretched out on the couch, eating grapes, and watching television all day while she was at school. "I know how hard you work, Grandma," she replied. Her comment surprised me.

You may feel guilty about not doing things right, or feel you should have done things differently with your own child. My feeling is that time has passed, what's done is done, and facts can't be changed.

When it comes to guilt, you have several options. Exploring guilt feelings in a support group is one. Try the group several times before you join. An experienced grandparent, one who has had the GRG job for years, may be willing to meet with you. It isn't necessary to spend hours with this person. Meeting for coffee may be all you need. Try not to tell long stories. Bring written questions with you to keep the conversation on track. Online support groups may also be helpful. Check the public library's self-help section for books about coping with guilt. AARP has made GRGs a top priority and posted many articles on its website.

Family Ethnicity and Culture

Ethnicity and culture are not the same. The word *ethnicity* refers to race, and the word *culture* refers to beliefs, values, and customs. I think of my home state of Minnesota when I think of ethnicity. Minnesota was mainly settled by Scandinavians and Germans. Customs and foods were passed from one generation to the next. At holiday time, many churches have lutefisk dinners—dried white fish soaked in water to hydrate it. The word *lutefisk* actually means "lye fish," an idea that scares me. Traditionalists think lutefisk tastes like any other fish, but I don't agree. *Lefse,* a traditional Norwegian pancake, is served with the lutefisk. Minnesotans turn out in droves to enjoy lutefisk dinners.

My family heritage is German and English. During my childhood years we didn't talk about culture, probably because we didn't know much about our family history. My father knew his family came from Manheim, Germany, and the names of a few relatives. My maternal grandmother came from Sheffield, England, when she was sixteen years old. Since my paternal grandmother died early, I never knew her. I'm glad my maternal grandmother lived until I was a senior in high school. She was a kind, hardworking woman, a mother of five children with needlework skills. I wish I knew more about my heritage, but the family Bible disappeared.

While I didn't like lefse and lutefisk, I did like several traditional British and German dishes, which were probably the biggest influences of my British and German heritage. Yorkshire pudding (a British recipe that's really a popover recipe rather than a pudding like the name implies) was a staple at our home, and I always looked forward to it. My mother learned how to make the recipe from her mother, and I learned it from my mother. In honor of my father's heritage, my mother often fixed German fried potatoes, and they were good.

From my mother, I learned to have a "stiff upper lip," as the Brits call it—no complaining, be cheerful, have a "cuppa," and carry on. From my father, a person who approached problems methodically, I learned to be careful, gather facts, and choose the best solution. The most valuable thing I learned from my father is persistence. He never gave up, and I try to follow his example.

Ethnicity and culture influence how you raise your grandchild. "How Culture Influences Health Beliefs," an article written for nurses, describes how the oldest male in Asian and Pacific families is the decision maker. This person is also the family spokesperson. Indian and Pakistani families tend to mistrust negative medical diagnoses, according to the article, because it reduces the chances of getting married. The article also says Vietnamese families use mystical beliefs to explain physical and mental illness. (No mention of biracial families was made.) The article provides a snapshot of how culture and ethnicity will affect how children and grandchildren are raised.

Guilt was mentioned previously and it turns up again here. Guilt can be a problem for all races. According to the National Grandparents Raising Grandchildren Examiner website, it's a special problem for African Americans. Author Kathy Gaillard writes about guilt in her article, "More African American Grandparents Are Raising Grandchildren." She thinks African Americans have an unspoken concept of "take care of your own." Many cultures have this belief. John and I took care of our own, and that's what you are doing.

Some of your family beliefs and customs may stand out from others. You don't have to pass on all of this knowledge to your grandchild immediately. Waiting to share beliefs until your grandchild is able to understand them is a better option. Giving your grandchild a sense of family is what's important. Family history is something to pass on to your grandchild. Stories will help your grandchild remember this history.

When you care for a grandchild, you are making family history. To document it, you may keep a diary, journal, or log. Everyone is an author in the computer age. This book documents a segment of my family history. Generations from now, a family member may be curious about this time and read it. Years from now, a family member may be curious about your family history and read your loving, meaningful words.

Maybe you're raising a grandchild because of your child's physical illness, mental illness, divorce, addiction, incarceration, military deployment, or death. In the foreword of this book, Kenneth J. Doka, PhD, describes grandparents who are raising their grandchildren as "wounded healers." This term fits me and may fit you. GRGs have many common feelings and some have common lives. Still, each grandparent is unique. There's no grandparent in the world exactly like you. Family pride may become your grandchild's pride, a way of living, and a path to the future.

What Works

1. Learn more about the GRG trend.
2. Focus on the joys of your role.
3. Foster your grandchild's friendships.
4. Watch for emotional problems and get help for your grandchild if necessary.
5. Stay out of divorce squabbles.
6. Remember, you're the adult in this relationship.
7. Get rid of guilt.
8. Respect your grandchild's ethnicity and culture.
9. Keep a diary, journal, or log.
10. Join a grandparenting support group.

CHAPTER 2

Grandparents Make Sacrifices

The instant you agreed to raise your grandchild, life changed. You may still see this moment in your mind and feel the feelings you felt then. At the time, you didn't realize how many sacrifices you would make. Some sacrifices are just that, while others turn out to be compromises.

John and I were glad to have the twins move into our house, but we knew we would sacrifice our privacy and some space. We were using our grandson's room as a storage room, and I had to move everything out of the packed closet. Our granddaughter's room was a guest room, and it couldn't be used for guests anymore. Our lifestyle changed, too, and we had little time to spend with friends. Still, we were glad to make these changes. Changes and sacrifices are inevitable for grandparents raising grandchildren.

Before the twins moved in with us, John had retired officially from Mayo Clinic. His department had a huge party for him at the Foundation House, a famous building in Rochester. Colleagues spoke about him, I spoke about him, and he was presented with a handsome photo montage of his father, brother, and himself—all of them Mayo Clinic physicians. It was a joyful, memorable evening. What an amazing group of friends!

But retirement didn't "fit" John, and he returned to his medical practice on a contract basis. He loved working with colleagues and, as usual, shared stories of unusual diagnoses while keeping confidentiality. A month or so later, John realized he would have to retire forever due to his new guardianship responsibilities. While I was managing the household, school connections, and activities, John was managing six estates—the twins', his mother's, his father's, and ours—and the paperwork was daunting.

Final retirement changed John's self-image. "I'm not a doctor anymore," he lamented. I told him he was still a doctor and would always be a doctor, but I don't think he believed me. In John's mind, he wasn't a doctor if he wasn't going to Mayo Clinic every day.

My story is slightly different. A freelance writer for decades, I had a home office, plenty of writing projects, plenty of gratis jobs, and many volunteer positions. But the twins' school hours didn't mesh with my schedule. Since I couldn't change school hours, I changed my writing hours. Instead of getting up at six in the morning, I got up at five and wrote in my pajamas for an hour. I stopped writing to fix breakfast for the twins. While John drove them to school, I showered, dressed for the day, and resumed writing. During the seven years the twins lived with us I cranked out many books and articles. Writing gave me a purpose and intellectual stimulation, two things I needed to be happy.

Change isn't always negative and may turn out to be positive. I still write early in the morning, when the house is so quiet I can almost hear it breathe, when my mind is racing and filled with words, and when my energy is high. Whether it's sunny, cloudy, raining, or snowing, early morning is a time of discovery. When I first adjusted my schedule, I enjoyed watching the day begin, seeing the light change, witnessing the sunrise, and observing wildlife. From my office window I saw birds, wild turkeys, herds of deer, an occasional flock of pheasants, stray rabbits, and a mallard or two. The window framed nature's ongoing drama, and I was fortunate to see it.

What are your sacrifices? You may have had to update a bathroom, give up storage space, resign from organizations, ignore hobbies, limit contacts with friends, or cancel an adult education class. Your list of sacrifices may be surprisingly long. Although you have made sacrifices, you are gaining days with a beloved grandchild. Sacrifices are nothing when compared to this. Every day, every hour, every moment is precious, and this time of life will never come again.

Loss of Peace and Quiet

Everyone needs a break now and then. You may dream of sitting in a cozy chair, leafing through a magazine or reading a book. No noise. No distractions. No time limit. When grandparents talk about retirement, they talk about a slower pace, time for hobbies, and travel dreams. Grandparents raising their grandkids are on the job twenty-four hours a day, seven days a week, and have little peace and quiet. Tiredness is more than a complaint; it becomes a way of life. There's no time off, only time on, a fact that makes some grandparents resentful.

You may drive your grandchild to and from school, for example, and get up earlier than before. If your grandchild is a teenager, you may struggle to stay awake until she or he comes home from a dance. You can't change the circumstances; you can only change yourself. How can you cope with the loss of peace and quiet?

Start by modifying your daily schedule. I've already told you that I modified mine by waking up earlier to write. Afternoons were so busy that I didn't do any new writing. Instead, I emailed people in the book industry and made phone calls. Take some time to brainstorm on how you can make your schedule easier.

One thing you can do is put "Me Time" on your schedule. I tried to do something for myself every day. Reading for pleasure, not research, was one of those things. I also watched my favorite decorating program on television. Your "Me Time" may include knitting, chatting with a friend, or puttering in the garden.

Try to have fifteen quiet minutes each day. You may be able to do this while your grandchild is napping, or while your grandchild is at school. Fifteen minutes isn't much time, yet it can be rejuvenating. You may want to lie down during this time to rest your legs or meditate for a few minutes.

Lower Income and Poverty

After the twins moved in with us, our living costs changed markedly. John and I were used to light meals—a small piece of fish, a crusty roll, and salad. Suddenly, I was cooking for growing teenagers who ate three times as much as we did. Since frozen meals, mixes, and kits are expensive, I made everything from scratch. If you're a "from scratch" cook, you know it takes more time.

I went to the grocery store more often. To get better car mileage, I made sure the tires were filled with air. Grocery store day was often errand day as well. Planning my driving routes also saved money. I went to stores on the north side of town one day, and stores on the south side of town the next.

Because the twins were of different sexes, we gave them their own bedrooms. Fortunately, we had enough space to do this. Shortly after the twins moved in, I hired a painter to touch up the bedroom walls. Our granddaughter's bedroom, the largest one in the house, was a charming guest room, with an antique, wrought iron bed, a white Parson's table, and a white wicker chair. Although these were attractive pieces, they weren't practical for a high school student. Our granddaughter asked us for a desk. We bought her an assemble-it-yourself desk and combination bookshelf.

Helen slept in the wrought iron bed when she was a child. Although I can't prove this, I think the bed linked our granddaughter with her mother.

Our grandson used the same bed his mother used as an adult and seemed to like it. He didn't need much for his bedroom. I bought a new bedspread, hung a wildlife print over his bed, and gave him a lamp from my office. When I stepped back and surveyed the room, it looked like a teenage boy's room, and that was good.

We expected these expenses, but others turned out to be a surprise. For example, we had a large awning installed over the deck to turn it into an outside room that we wouldn't have installed if our grandchildren hadn't lived with us. Our grandson and his friends grilled hot dogs on the deck and sat around and talked. Because the twins needed more privacy, we bought a sleeper sofa for the lower level. The twins spent lots of time downstairs with their friends. Seeing the twins having a good time with their friends and hearing their laughter made John and me smile.

When we bought the house, we didn't know it would suit our grandfamily. The kitchen, dining room, living room, and family room were on the first floor. Three bedrooms and two bathrooms were on the top floor. A fourth bedroom, which I used as an office, a bathroom, and another family room were on the lower level. Maintaining a comfortable temperature in a three-level house turned out to be a problem, especially during the winter, so we installed a high-efficiency thermostat.

On winter nights we set the thermostat at sixty-eight degrees; during the day we set it at seventy degrees. To conserve heat, we lowered the thermal shades as soon as the daylight began to fade. These steps didn't make our granddaughter's room any warmer, and she complained about the cold. Maybe the heat wasn't getting to her bedroom, we figured, so we closed a duct in our bedroom and another in our grandson's bedroom. Our granddaughter was still cold. Two months later, as spring approached, I checked the window in her bedroom and discovered it was open several inches. We had been heating Rochester, Minnesota, for weeks.

You may be concerned about your heating and cooling bills. Get your furnace checked if you think your bills are too high. State offices may be able to help. Minnesota has a heating assistance program, and your state may have one too. Some heating companies have a subscription service—an automatic furnace check before winter. In the long run, this service could save you money.

A CBS News website article "For Grandfamilies, Raising Grandkids Can Mean Going Broke" details some of the financial challenges grandparents face, including higher food bills. Researchers don't know if grandfamily homes have less income because grandparents aren't working anymore, or if the family was low-income before the grandparents became caregivers. The shortage of funds depends, in part, on money management. From what I read and see on television, most Americans aren't saving money. John and I are frugal people, and this habit gave us enough money to care for our grandkids.

This may be a good time to review your income and expenses. Do you take steps to save money? Have you talked with a financial advisor?

The US Department of Health and Human Services on Women's Health cites funding sources in its website article "Healthy Again: Raising Children Again." Available funding includes Temporary Assistance for needy Families (TANF), Supplemental Security Income, Social Security, Women, Infants and Children program (WIC), Medicaid, and guardianship subsidies. Benefits vary from state to state, so contact your state government for more information. Ask for forms, pamphlets, or booklets when you email or call.

You may have moved to cheaper housing to save money. Still, money is short. According to a New Media website article, "Millions Are Raising Their Grandkids in Poverty," some grandkids are raised by aunts, uncles, adult siblings, and family friends. The article describes this arrangement as an "informal child welfare system" and claims this system cares for ten to twelve times more children than the foster care system. While this sounds negative, it's reality for many GRGs and GAPs.

Just when they need money most, grandparents may cut back on work hours or retire early to care for grandkids. This is a huge financial adjustment. To pay their bills, these grandparents may dip into retirement funds again and again. Richard Eisenberg makes this point in his article, "Grandparents Raising Grandkids: Money Squeeze." Financial help is available from the Supplemental Nutrition Assistance Program, formerly known as food stamps. Ongoing financial worries and woes like these can fracture a marriage.

Marriage Problems

Marriage care takes time, something you're short on as a grandparent raising your grandchildren. A marriage can limp along for months but will continue to deteriorate unless you take action. The only people who can rescue a marriage are the ones pledged to each other.

The American Association for Marriage and Family Therapy (AAMFT), in its article "Grandparents Raising Grandchildren," says grandparents who are raising grandkids have less time for themselves. You may have planned a romantic dinner at a popular restaurant, only to discover your grandchild has the flu. I wanted time for writing, and it was hard to find. John missed me if I served his breakfast and went downstairs to write. He missed me if I wrote after dinner. While I was writing, I missed him too. So I juggled my hours, and this gave me more time with John. A close marriage still needs care, and you can do this by making care a priority.

In the same article cited above, AAMFT says lack of time can be stressful and cause feelings of anger, grief, and loss. John and I didn't have any marriage problems, thank goodness, although we lost the ability to go out to dinner on a whim, attend conferences like we used to, and spend time with friends.

A year after the twins moved in, we felt like we needed a break. We decided to attend a conference and made arrangements for the twins to stay with people we knew and trusted while we were gone. The idea of having some time alone almost made us giddy. We flew to Los Angeles, California, and attended the Aerospace Medical Association conference there. Seeing old friends was fun, and we enjoyed the local tours. I belonged to the Wing of the Aerospace Medical Association and am still a member. Wing tours are always great and in L.A. we took a behind the scenes tour of a movie studio.

For the first time in months, John and I slowed down and spent time with each other. Going out to dinner felt like a first date. We compared feelings, challenges, and discussed future plans. When we returned to Rochester we felt refreshed, energized, and ready to return to GRG responsibilities.

Because we've been married a long time, John and I knew marriage required effort. I'm blessed to have a husband who shares his feelings. We use "I feel" statements and praise each other often.

Saying "I love you" is part of every day. Silence bothers some couples, but it doesn't bother us. John has thanked me many times for not "being one of those wives who talks all the time."

John and I tried to be in bed by ten o'clock. Many GRGs are so tired they can hardly think. These dedicated grandparents yearn for the luxury of a good night's sleep. Even if they take steps to get a good night's sleep, they may not get it because their minds keep mulling over problems. Interrupted sleep isn't restorative sleep.

To keep your marriage strong, you may wish to write "night out" on the calendar. Do something different, such as going to a craft show, an unusual art exhibit, or the newest ethnic restaurant in town. When you're there, turn off your cell phone and don't check it. Pay attention to the person you love and the joy of being together.

Some grandparents end up staying together for their grand-child only. Things didn't start out this way, however. In the first months of being a GRG, these grandparents worked together and enjoyed it. But the daily grind, the same old, same old, eventually caught up with them. Tomorrow doesn't sound exciting when you're trying to get through today. Fatigue takes a toll, and these grandparents may have little energy to put into marriage. All of their energy is directed at their grandchild. If your marriage is headed this way, stop and think about why you married in the first place. What attracted you to your partner? What attracted your partner to you? With effort, gentle care, and expressions of love, the qualities you admired in your partner may become visible again.

A grandchild's feelings can impact a marriage. Our goal was to get the twins through this dark time, support school activities, and foster their dreams. Our granddaughter had been on the gymnastics team for several years. Shortly after she moved in with us, the team held a parents' night. Thankfully, our granddaughter gave us a "heads up" about this. "Someone will say your names and I'll give you a flower," she explained. That sounded simple enough. When the girls lined up for the ceremony, our granddaughter was first.

The girls had lined up by height. Our granddaughter, the shortest person on the team, looked like a toy in comparison to her tall teammates. Some people in the audience may have thought she was there by mistake. The announcer introduced us as her grandparents. No other grandparents were introduced, only parents, and we wondered if this bothered our granddaughter. She walked toward us and handed each of us a rose. John and I wanted to cry because we missed Helen so much. Yet we were glad to be there, cheering for our granddaughter.

Some grandkids that live with their grandparents face a stigma. Classmates may make hurtful statements such as, "You live with those old folks?" A grandchild doesn't have many responses to hurtful statements. Options include ignoring the statement, countering it with a positive statement, or getting angry. Citing some facts may be the best approach, such as:

"My grandpa makes the best apple pie!"

"We have fun together. On Saturday we're going to an ice skating show."

"I know I can always count on my grandparents."

When our grandson was twenty-five years old, I asked him if any of his classmates had made hurtful comments. "Nobody ever made a derogatory comment and, looking back, I'm guessing if somebody had they would have been immediately ostracized," he replied. My grandson went on to say he was never embarrassed to live with us and was "happy to have a home."

GRGs are raising grandchildren because of love, and we can be proud of that. Unfortunately, this is a role that can create loneliness and isolation.

Loneliness, Isolation, and Depression

Ask grandparents what bothers them, and most will say loneliness. Ongoing tasks leave grandparents little time for self-care. You look so busy that friends may stop inviting you to lunch, bowling, or other events. Gradually, you lose contact with the outside world. The lack of social contacts can lead to loneliness. Although social contacts can be maintained via email and Skype, after the email is sent and the Skype call is over, you're still in one place, and friends are in another. Most of my friends knew my story and were thinking of me, yet I rarely saw them. This wasn't their fault, it was mine, due to my daily schedule:

5:00 a.m. Get up, make coffee, and start writing.

6:00 a.m. Stop writing. Fix breakfast for family. (I often made a coffee cake.)

7:30 a.m. Shower and get ready for day. Start laundry. Resume writing.

9:30 or 10:00 a.m. Grocery shopping, run errands.

12:00 noon. Eat a quick lunch. Proofread previous writing.

1:00 p.m. Do more laundry. Put folded laundry away. Pay bills. Work. Prep for dinner.

2:00 p.m. Vacuum, dust, make book industry contacts.

3:00 p.m. Pick up twins from school. Run errands with twins.

5:00 p.m. Start dinner. Cook extra for tomorrow's meals.

6:30 to 9:00 p.m. School activities: gymnastics, concerts, etc.

9:30 or 10:00 p.m. Set table for tomorrow's breakfast. Go to bed.

I ran into a friend at the grocery store and asked her what was new in her life. She had just returned from three weeks in Europe and shared a story about her trip. "What's new with you?" she asked in return. Nothing was the true answer, although I didn't say this. I mumbled something about our grandchildren's school events and changed the subject. The truth was, I had little to say. Telling her I went to the grocery store every other day didn't compare to a European trip. The contrast between our lives couldn't have been sharper. On the way home, I realized loneliness was my new normal.

Loneliness walked in the door when your grandchild walked in the door. You agreed to care for a precious, vulnerable, wounded grandchild, not to become a lonely, isolated person. As time passes, grandparenting can make you feel trapped, with no end in sight. You need to take action if isolation has become a problem. Loneliness can lead to the blues, and the blues can lead to depression, a real medical illness.

John and I had to sort feelings of grief from feelings of loneliness. This required effort. We finally decided our sadness was grief, not depression, and this proved to be true. Depression is common in family caregivers. In its article "Caregiver Depression: Prevention Counts," Mayo Clinic says feelings of sadness, loneliness, and guilt can trigger depression. This isn't the same as having a bad day. The article lists the symptoms of depression. Below, I paraphrased some of the symptoms, edited some of the wording, and added my comments.

- **Feeling sad, empty, and hopeless.** This can happen even if you're usually an upbeat person. You may start to worry about yourself. Self-worry is an awful feeling.

- **Angry outbursts.** Your outbursts may surprise family members and you. This isn't like you, which adds to your list of worries. You may say things during your outbursts that you will regret later.

- **No interest in normal activities.** In the past, you may have enjoyed several hobbies and/or sports. You haven't maintained these interests, and the unused tennis racket sits in a closet.

- **Sleep problems.** These problems include interrupted sleep, fitful sleep, and sleep deprivation. Poor sleep affects your thinking, coordination, and reaction time. Consult a physician or nurse practitioner if sleep problems persist.

- **Lack of energy.** You used to be energetic. Now you're lagging and struggling to get things done. The to-do list has become a not-done list.

- **Changes in appetite.** These changes include no interest in food, overeating, and snacking too much. You may be eating too many salty and sugary foods.

- **Anxious, restless feelings.** You keep waiting for something to happen. Constant anxiety makes you more nervous.

- **Slowed thinking, speech, and coordination.** Framing sentences takes more time and you move slowly. You're developing an "I don't care" attitude and it's worrisome.

- **Concentration problems.** This includes things like losing your car keys and doing odd things, such as putting a comb in the refrigerator. (Yes, I've done this.)

- **Thoughts of death and suicide.** These are depression red flags. Have you had any suicidal thoughts? If so, have you shared them with anyone?

- **Unexplained physical problems.** You may start to have headaches and stomach aches. Although you don't know what's wrong, you know you aren't yourself.

Loneliness is the body's warning system. Just as a tornado siren warns you to take shelter immediately, loneliness warns you to take action—the sooner the better. Persistent loneliness is harmful to your health. Don't be ashamed to ask your doctor, religious leader, or a certified counselor for help. Asking for help shows that you're a self-aware, proactive person. Your caregiving journey doesn't have to be a solitary journey.

As Gail Sheehy advises in her book *Passages in Caregiving*, don't be a lonely hero or heroine. Heroic caregivers tend to see what they want to see, Sheehy explains, and this can lead to poor decisions. You may also miss some important facts. Sheehy thinks we need to do something for ourselves every day to counter the loneliness of caregiving. Think about how you take care of yourself. The list may include family dinners, pursuing hobbies, attending church suppers, singing in a choir, enjoying the arts in your community, and taking adult education courses.

I take care of myself with reading, cooking, music, and writing. Interestingly, many of my friends don't think writing is self-care. Well, it is, and I love writing so much I do it in my sleep. I'm grateful for this ability, and I will continue to write as long as my mind works. Writing helps me and others too.

Because I'm a self-help and spirituality writer, I'm doing research and learning all the time. One thing I learned is that I have to prepare for holidays.

Holidays can sidetrack grandparents like you and me. A blogger on caregiving.com expands on this idea in her post "Caregiving Conversations: Caregiver Loneliness During the Holidays." You may not have much time for yourself at holiday time, the author notes, "and get so busy you miss family gatherings." Her solutions are to simplify family meals, ask for gift buying and wrapping help, and simplify traditions.

Mayo Clinic created a tradition for the bereaved—a free holiday concert for hospice families. I was asked if I would be willing to speak at one concert and write something for concert attendees. I agreed and wrote "My Holiday Survival Kit," a pocket card people could refer to later. Several points on the card may be applied to your life as a GRG or GAP. The points include the following: 1) Have one meaningful conversation each day; 2) Promise to be kind to myself; 3) Attend a few special events and note them on the calendar; and 4) Add physical activity to my daily routine.

Health Changes and Challenges

Grandparents in their sixties and beyond may develop health problems as a result of caregiving. "The Health and Well-Being of Grandparents Caring for Grandchildren," an article by the Population Reference Bureau, summarizes the impact of caregiving on health. I selected several key findings to share.

- When compared to non-caregivers, grandparents raising grandchildren have more health problems: depression, coronary heart disease, limited activity, asthma, and diabetes.
- New grandparent caregivers (those who have been doing it for less than two years) are less likely to get preventive health care.
- A study of four hundred Ohio grandmothers who moved from a lower level of care [babysitting, weekend care, five days a week] to primary care worsened their physical health.
- Poverty affects the health of GRGs and is linked to higher rates of pneumonia and influenza. (This may be due to lack of health insurance, no health insurance, or lack of transportation.)

Caregiving was physically taxing for me because I have arthritic hips and lived in a three-level house. Rochester is home base for Mayo Clinic, and we take advantage of this. We get the shots we're supposed to and keep our prescriptions current. If we need immediate care, we go to Community Medicine. Our bills are automatically sent to Medicare and Tricare for Life, coverage for military personal. Grandparents without health insurance, or those with poor health plans, may neglect their health. This isn't good for them or their grandchildren.

Sleep has a profound effect on overall health. According to an article by Barry C. Jacobs, "4 Tips for Better Sleep While Caregiving," too little sleep has been associated with increased appetite, anxiety, depression, traffic accidents, and memory problems. Jacobs gives four suggestions for getting better sleep, and I added comments from my caregiving experience.

1. Sleep in a separate room from your grandchild. Fix up your room for sleep. Use comfortable bedding, darken the room, and lower the temperature. Remove the television if there is one in the room.

2. Dump worries during an "anxious hour." Jacobs thinks you should worry during daytime hours, not nighttime, and put your worries in writing. This step may help you cast worries aside and get some sleep.

3. Develop a sleep routine and good sleep habits. Avoid alcohol because it will wake you up later. Try to go to bed at the same time each night and get up at the same time each morning.

4. Try deep breathing. Breathing slowly helps to slow your heart rate. Diaphragm breathing also helps.

With adequate sleep, at least seven hours a night, life looks brighter, and you have more energy. Yet many GRGs don't get the sleep they need. Your actions may be interfering with sleep, according to Sheryl Kraft, author of "8 Surprising Sleep Stealers" posted on the American Grandparents Association website. The sleep stealers are e-readers (the blue light interferes with melatonin production), being overweight, certain medications, taking a warm bath before bed, fatty and salty foods, bedroom clutter, exercising too late, and stress.

Never-ending GRG tasks can lead to a rise in blood pressure. Hypertension can be a hidden problem, and you may not know you have it. See a physician or nurse practitioner if your blood pressure hasn't been taken recently. Your health professional will be able to tell you the target blood pressure for your age. You can track your own pressure with a cuff purchased from a discount store.

For the well-being of family members, compile a list of emergency phone numbers. Enter the numbers into your cell phone, or post them by your landline phone. While you're at it, determine how long it takes to drive from your place to the hospital. Locate the entrance and find out where to park. Also find out if valet service is available.

Compare Losses and Gains

When you're tired and still have tasks to do, it's easy to slip into negative thinking. You may focus on the sacrifices you've made, not on the benefits of your sacrifices. To help you stay positive, it may help to compare your losses and gains. Gains can come from losses. For one thing, you are getting to know your grandchild, a true blessing that many grandparents don't have. You have a front-row seat to your grandchild's growth and development. You are participating in shared activities with your grandchild. One of the biggest gains is planning a future together. I think grandparenting gains outweigh the losses.

Lenora M. Poe, PhD, a marriage, family, and child therapist in Berkeley, California, describes losses and gains in her article "Connecting the Bridges: Grandparenting Grandchildren."

Poe thinks grandparents can become emotionally overwhelmed, and I agree with her. After I read her article, I made a personal comparison list, with losses on the left, and gains on the right. I made this list early in my grandparenting journey. When I was revising this book I read the list again and was pleased to see it was still true. You can make a similar list.

SOME OF MY LOSSES	SOME OF MY GAINS
Loss of a quiet house	My granddaughter has a clear, pure voice. Hearing her practice choir music was a joy. Hearing my grandson play his father's guitar was also a joy. Drums were another story.
Lack of privacy	Our house had an ideal layout for a grandfamily. The twins closed their bedroom doors when they wanted privacy, and we closed ours.
Hurried dinners due to school activities	I enjoyed the school activities, especially the gymnastics meets, band, and choir concerts.
No spur of the moment activities	The time I spent with the twins helped me to know them, understand them, and feel close to them.
Waiting to use laundry equipment	The twins did their own laundry, which helped me, and helped them in college.
Fewer social contacts; loneliness	I made a difference in the twins' lives. I suspected this years ago, and know it now.
Energy drain and fatigue	The twins appreciated my efforts. Thankfully, after twelve years in the classroom, I knew how to pace myself.

When I compared my losses and gains, an important truth became clear: John and I provided a home for the twins. You're doing the same thing now. Children need to know they have a home to return to, according to Poe, and "someone there to receive them, a bed to sleep in, a table to sit at and eat at, and someone to hug and say, 'I love you. You are special.'" We provided these things for the twins. In the future, if something happens to one of us, the other will stay connected with the twins and offer advice when asked.

A grandparent's love of a grandchild never ends. Our grand-daughter is married now, yet we keep her well-being in mind. Our grandson has a girlfriend and we include her in family activities. That's what GRGs and GAPs do. The following tips come from my caregiving experience.

What Works

1. Take steps to lower household bills.

2. Put marriage care on the calendar.

3. Counter isolation with social contacts and self-care.

4. Make "Me Time" part of each day.

5. Practice self-care.

6. Prepare for the holidays.

7. Make your health a top priority.

8. Get a good night's sleep.

9. Watch for symptoms of depression.

10. Measure your blood pressure.

11. Make a losses and gains comparison chart

CHAPTER 3

Why You Are Grieving

Rabbi Grollman called me about the first version of this book. During our conversation he said, "Every grandparent raising their grandchildren is grieving for something." His comment was the seed for this chapter. Grief and I are well acquainted—too well acquainted. I'm a bereaved parent, daughter, sibling, niece, cousin, friend, and pet owner.

Our experiences with grief change us; we aren't the same people we used to be. Life feels more precious, more fragile, and we are grateful to be alive.

"But I'm not grieving," you may declare. If you look closely, however, you may realize that you are grieving for something. You may be grieving because of lost dreams, poor health, chronic illness, financial worries, lack of friends, and even yourself. Things weren't supposed to be this way at this time of life. Non-death experiences can be powerful and have a cumulative effect on your life. Some shadows of grief are long and have existed for months or years. For example, you may wish you had confronted your adult child about drug use and intervened on behalf of your grandchild sooner. Other shadows, such as a silly argument best forgotten, can be cast aside.

Shadows of Grief

Your grief may be apparent to others or hidden from everyone, including yourself. I wished I could turn back the clock to a happier time, when my daughter, father-in-law, brother, and former son-in-law were alive. If this were possible, the twins would have two parents to love and care for them. Unfortunately, time can't be reversed. You are raising grandkids now, living a new life, and coping with new challenges.

Before, your grandchild may have come for birthday parties, holiday dinners, and stayed overnight every once in a while. Then you became a GRG and your occasional role became a full-time role. This is a difficult adjustment for you and your grandchild. Raising a grandchild takes tremendous energy, and your energy may be sparse. Friends may have already drifted away, and you fear they won't be back. You need friends, need to socialize with them and count on them. Will the phrase "out of sight, out of mind" apply to you?

You may have suffered the loss of a supportive family. When you first became a GRG, family members praised you. Then some criticized you and you felt wounded. Who can you count on if you can't count on family?

Raising a special-needs grandchild, one with a chronic illness, learning problems, attention deficit disorder (ADD), or post traumatic stress disorder (PTSD) increases your grandparenting responsibilities. If your grandchild lived with an abusive family and saw and heard things no child should see or hear, she or he may develop PTSD. This fact can cause you to grieve for your grandchild. Your grief may increase when you realize your grandchild is grieving too. Whether spoken or silent, your grandchild may grapple with a painful question: Why did this happen to me?

Caring for a child with relocation stress syndrome (RSS) can be a challenge as well. RSS is a physical and/or psychological disturbance resulting from the transfer from one place to another. The syndrome, originally applied to nursing home residents, can be applied to your situation. Your grandchild was forced to move. Moving was stressful but was just the beginning. Now your grandchild has to adjust to a different room, sleep in a strange bed, eat unfamiliar food, and adapt to a new routine. RSS can cast a shadow of grief on a child's life. She or he may mourn the loss of friends or the old neighborhood with its nearby park. Your challenge as a GRG or GAP is to try and make up for these losses. You may take your child to a different park, point out the advantages of your neighborhood, and invite new friends over.

Losing touch with hobbies can cast a shadow of grief for you. Golf clubs are stashed in a closet, and you don't know if you'll use them again. Other hobbies may have disappeared, and you miss them. Will you lose the skills you worked so hard to attain?

Finally, the loss of dreams casts a shadow. This point was mentioned before and is worth mentioning again. Grandparents who are raising their grandchildren have many losses, and each one sparks grief. Early on, when the twins had just moved in with us, I was somewhat robotic as I went about my daily tasks. The death of four family members had taken joy from my life. I worried a lot. Multiple losses put my mind on constant alert for trouble.

Worry isn't all bad, however, and keeps us on our toes. Because of worry, we make sure doors and windows are locked before going to bed. We check and recheck plans because of worry. We stock up on first-aid supplies in case they are needed. Helpful as worry can be, it can become excessive and make you feel like you've lost control of your life. Loss of control causes stress, and you may be stressed already. You may be grieving, and that creates emotional pain and long-term stress.

Types of Grief

If you're grieving while raising a grandchild, be on the lookout for grief detours. There are many types of grief. There isn't room here to explain all of the types, so I've selected those that may affect you. If you think your "normal" grief is becoming something else, contact a physician or grief counselor. Life is complicated right now, and you don't need grief to add to your complications.

Delayed grief. With this form of grief, feelings are pushed to the back of the mind. It happens because humans can only handle so much, according to Judy Tatelbaum, author of *The Courage to Grieve*. According to Tatelbaum we may delay grief in order to function, and this is understandable.

Exaggerated grief. Also called chronic grief, this type of grief can linger for years. Instead of focusing on life, the person focuses on death. The grieving person obsesses on the deceased, thinks about them all the time, talks about them constantly, and becomes morbid. Some people talk about the deceased in the present tense, as if the person were still living. A person with exaggerated grief is stuck in the past, and this isn't healthy.

Complicated grief. This is a heightened, ongoing state of mourning. Mayo Clinic describes this grief in a website article, "Complicated Grief." This form of grief has many symptoms, such as feeling that life has no meaning. Things can get so bad that the person with complicated grief thinks about suicide. "Call your doctor if you've recently lost a loved one and feel such profound disbelief, hopelessness, or intense yearning for your loved one that you can't function in daily life," Mayo Clinic advises.

Disenfranchised grief. According to the Free Dictionary, this type of grief can't be publicly acknowledged because it can't be publicly expressed. If a loved one died of AIDS, for example, family members may not want to admit or publicize this fact because they fear an "it's your own fault" response. Other examples include the death of a grandchild, death of an adopted child, a miscarriage, or death of a former spouse.

Anticipatory grief. Everyone experiences this type of grief, yet many have never heard the term. Anticipatory grief is a feeling of loss before a death or dreaded event occurs. This type of grief is powerful and worthy of more discussion.

Anticipatory Grief

Anticipatory grief is awful, and follows you like a dark cloud. You can't escape it. How does anticipatory grief relate to raising your grandchild? If your adult child (the parent of your grandchild) has a debilitating disease, you will feel anticipatory grief. What if the disease accelerates? How will your grandchild respond?

If your grandchild's parent is addicted to hard drugs or prescription drugs, you will feel anticipatory grief. Like a flashing neon sign, the words *overdose* and *death* keep flashing in your mind. Getting involved in a bitter custody fight can also spark anticipatory grief. What will happen to your grandchild if you lose? Discovering that your grandchild has epilepsy, or another disease, can prompt anticipatory grief feelings. Thinking about your grandchild's future makes you sad, and you hope the seizures can be controlled.

The death of four family members made me fearful of another family member dying. I wondered what would become of me if one of the twins died in a car crash, a common cause of death in teens.

In 2004 I wrote a book titled *Smiling Through Your Tears: Anticipating Grief*. Lois Krahn, MD, a Mayo Clinic psychiatrist and sleep expert, is the co-author. She called me shortly after the book was released. "Before we worked on the book I didn't think about anticipatory grief very much," Dr. Krahn admitted. "Now I realize it walks into my office every day." Anticipatory grief doesn't have the shock of death, but it can still be a shock. Since anticipatory grief can linger for months or years, it's wise to be alert to its symptoms:

- Denial
- Emotional numbness
- Nervous, restless behavior
- Ongoing anxiety and dread
- Mood swings
- Crying spells and a choked feeling in the throat
- Persistent feelings of sadness
- Depression
- Anger
- Ambivalent feelings
- Inability to concentrate and poor retention
- Constant forgetfulness
- Disorganized, confused behavior

- Increased vulnerability
- Health changes
- Hyperactivity
- Poor eating habits
- Sleep problems
- Fatigue and/or exhaustion
- Feeling disconnected and alone

Dr. Krahn and I wrote our book for readers who were anticipating the death of a loved one. As you can see, almost every symptom can be applied to grandparents who are raising grandchildren. You may have developed many of these symptoms, a fact that makes you uncomfortable. Why is anticipatory grief so powerful?

For one thing, your thoughts jump around like crazy. You think about the past, present, and future all at once. Conflicting thoughts can make you worry about yourself. Friends may notice you have changed and wonder if you have a psychological problem. You don't have a problem; you are grieving.

You feel sorrow and hope simultaneously. This may be the most unique aspect of anticipatory grief. Perhaps the doctor made the wrong diagnosis—a hopeful thought. Deep in your heart, you hope a cure will be developed for your loved one's disease, yet you continue to fear the worst.

Every day is a day of uncompleted loss. Toward the end of my mother's life, when I awakened, I wondered if this would be the day she would die. An ongoing feeling of loss is a nerve-racking feeling. As it turned out, my post-death grief was shortened because my anticipatory grief was so long.

The time factor grinds you down physically and emotionally. Maybe you're trying to adopt your grandchild but don't know how long it will take. The adoption may be contested or denied.

If you're this worn out now, how will you feel a year from now? Two years from now? Family members may wonder why you're grieving. Explaining your feelings is hard because you can hardly track them yourself.

You're living with suspense and fear. In fact, these feelings become part of your life. Fearing that others won't understand, you keep your feelings to yourself. Grief experts call this "stuffing feelings," and you may feel stuffed with worry, insecurity, and sadness. Uncertainty rules your life.

Your grief can become complex. Therese A. Rando, PhD, author of the article "Anticipatory Grief: The Term Is a Misnomer but the Phenomenon Exists," thinks anticipatory grief imposes limits on our lives. You may be afraid to travel, for example, because your loved one could die while you're gone.

While anticipatory grief doesn't have the shock of sudden death, it's still a shock. One grief author compares anticipatory grief to an avalanche. I was shocked after my father-in-law died because what I feared had finally happened, and death is final.

Post-Death Grief

Grieving for four family members and raising the twins at the same time was the greatest challenge of my life. Memories of this time are a blur. However, some experiences, such as the twins graduating from high school with honors, are clear in my mind. A decade has passed since Helen died and I still grieve for her.

You have my deepest, heartfelt sympathy if you're grieving for the parent of your grandchild. The death of a child is an out-of-order death. Yet this is what happened. I couldn't change the plot of my story, but I could influence the ending, and have tried to make good things from grief. I wrote eight grief recovery books, spoke about grief recovery, and cared for the twins. One problem I had, and you may have, is crying in front of the grand-children.

John and I were reluctant to cry in front of the twins because we thought if we started crying, we might not be able to stop. Nevertheless, we did cry, and it was okay. From their perspective, not crying would be odd, almost as if we didn't care about or love their mother. We loved Helen and continue to love her. My experiences with grief have taught me that love is stronger than death, and this is comforting.

John and I tried to keep Helen's spirit alive. On the one-year anniversary of her death, we held a brief graveside ceremony for the family. I created a handout about Helen's legacy. The handout listed the kinds of values that can get anyone through life. Since the ceremony was held, the twins have moved, and they may not have their lists anymore. We still have our list and, as the years passed, it became more meaningful.

Helen's Values

Believe in a Higher Power.

Live your beliefs.

Stay on the AA path.

Family comes first.

Love and enjoy your children.

Get an education and keep learning.

Find an occupation that doesn't seem like work.

Share with others even if you have little to give.

Know what's important and what isn't.

Help others.

Laugh every day.

Making a similar list may help you cope with post-death grief. Although your grandchild may not appreciate it now, the list may become a treasure in years to come. Joining a grief organization may help you. I belong to the local chapter of The Compassionate Friends, an international organization for parents, siblings, and families that have suffered the death of a child. To learn more about this organization, visit compassionatefriends.org. In my experience, this is the only group that understands the losses I've suffered. The Compassionate Friends has a magazine, *We Need Not Walk Alone*, and puts on national and regional conferences.

You also need to think about yourself. Check your support system if you haven't done it recently. Friends may have moved away and organizations may have closed down.

Charles N. Seashore, PhD, describes the purposes and parts of a support system in his article "Developing and Using a Personal Support System." A well-developed, up-to-date support system includes a variety of people, Seashore notes, and isn't limited to those close to you, those who listen to you, or those who share your views. A support system is a resource pool that supports you, moves in the direction you choose, and leaves you feeling stronger. You need to choose support system people carefully. They could be role models, people who share your interests, close friends, helpers, and challengers "who can help motivate one to explore ways of doing things," Seashore explains.

Although Seashore doesn't think it's necessary to notify the people in your system, I think it's the right thing to do. Having a support system helps you recover from grief and care for your grandchildren. I created this checklist to help you evaluate your support system.

Grief Support System Checklist

My grief support system is current.
   Yes _____ No _____

It includes family members, friends, and spiritual/religious support.
   Yes _____ No _____

There are people of varying ages in my support system.
   Yes _____ No _____

All of the people in my support system are competent.
   Yes _____ No _____

Many of these people are role models.
   Yes _____ No _____

The people in my support system share my interests.
   Yes _____ No _____

The people in my support system have skills/contacts that enable them to act quickly.
   Yes _____ No _____

Different community groups are represented in my support system.
   Yes _____ No _____

I've looked into backup resources for my support system.
   Yes _____ No _____

A grief support group is part of my system.
   Yes _____ No _____

I've learned more about how children express grief.
   Yes _____ No _____

How Kids Express Their Grief

Adults understand the finality of death, yet it remains a mystery. We can only imagine how mysterious death is for children. According to the American Academy of Pediatrics, a child's understanding of death depends on their age and development. Elyse C. Salek, MEd and Kenneth R. Ginsburg, MD, MS Ed, FAAP make this point in their article, "How children Understand Death & What You Should Say." The authors cite four main concepts about death: irreversibility, finality, inevitability, and causality.

"Preschoolers see death as something temporary," write Salek and Ginsburg. Cartoons may reinforce this concept. Never tell a child that death is like going to sleep. This comparison can make them afraid of going to bed, afraid of falling asleep, and afraid they might die in their sleep. While kids become aware of death when a pet dies, it takes time to realize that a pet, loved one, or friend is never coming back. From my teaching experience, I know grieving preschoolers may resort to *magical thinking*, a mix of reality and fantasy.

You can help your grandchild by sticking to a routine, giving more hugs (ask permission first), speaking calmly, and providing comfort items—a snuggly quilt, teddy bear, or stuffed animal. Your grandchild may also benefit from a *linking object*—a watch, necklace, or scarf—something that connects her or him to the deceased.

"Bereavement Reactions by Age Group," an article on the Kids Health website, says preschool children may become clingy, irritable, or withdraw significantly (crawling, asking for a bottle, eating differently, rejecting food, complaining about food). You can help by sticking to a routine, reading comforting stories, increasing physical contact, and encouraging play. Providing art materials—plain paper, crayons, watercolor markers, colored pencils—is also helpful. I recommend the book, *When Something Terrible Happens: Children Can Learn to Cope with Grief* by art therapist Marge Heegaard. Check out the other therapy books she has written as well.

Elementary school children commonly respond to death with anxiety, irritability, clingy behavior, not wanting to go to school, physical complaints, bed wetting, and self-blame. An elementary-age child may become afraid of the dark. Your grandchild may start to have nightmares. A physically healthy grandchild may begin to complain of headaches, stomachaches, and muscle aches. You can help by sticking to a routine, helping them find words to describe their feelings, remaining calm, and encouraging play. For play items I recommend dolls, puppets, and art materials to make puppets. Be sure your grandchild gets plenty of outdoor play. Free time, or what used to be called free play, will help your grandchild sort things out and recover.

Go online and use the search words *children's grief* to find out more about age-specific responses to grief. The Children's Grief Education Association has an excellent chart that details responses according to age, starting with birth to age two, three to five years, six to nine years, nine to twelve years, and teenage years. Mary M. Lyles, MSW, LCSW, compiled the chart titled "Navigating Children's Grief: How to Help Following a Death" posted on childgrief.org.

School-age kids begin to understand that death is final, but not what caused death. Salek and Ginsberg offer recommendations that may be applied to grandparenting. They think it's important to assure your grandchild that every person who gets sick doesn't die. You might remind your grandchild of the time you were ill.

"Remember how I coughed and coughed? But I'm all better now." From my experience, you may have to reassure your grandchild of this several times.

Be honest about your own health. You don't have to supply every detail; a few will do. For example, you can say there's a difference between being tired after a busy day and being ill. I had cataract surgery on both eyes. After surgery on one eye, I wore a protective shield over my eye and looked like a robot. Rather than complaining about the shield, I joked about it. When I had the cataract removed from my other eye, the twins didn't comment because they were familiar with the recovery process.

Another suggestion is to remind your grandchild about the people who care for her or him. To reinforce this point, gather photos of these people and glue them on a poster for a young child. An older grandchild may create her or his own poster.

Take steps to reduce your grandchild's anxiety. For example, if talking about the deceased is painful, don't do it when your grandchild is present. Gradually, John and I were able to tell stories about our departed loved ones without crying. The twins were able to do this too, a sign of progress.

Practice self-care and tell your grandchild what you're doing. "I have a cold and am drinking lots of orange juice to feel better." You don't have to supply a detailed account of your self-care steps, just reassurance.

Like you, a grandchild will feel many emotions after a loved one dies. Arrange to see a grief counselor if your grandchild has sleep problems or becomes troublesome. Before you seek help, it may be a good idea to make a loss time line with your grandchild, something that many grief experts recommend.

Start by drawing a horizontal line across a piece of paper. List losses above the line starting with the earliest ones your grandchild can remember, such as the death of a dog. List the dates of these losses below the line. Some grief experts recommend listing losses and dates above the line, and feelings about these losses below the line. Personally, I think this visual should be as simple as possible. A young child who can't print may draw the line, and you can add the information.

Grieving teens often experience anger because the person who died "really screwed up their life," according to Dr. Heidi Horsley and Dr. Gloria Horsley, authors of *Teen Grief Relief*. The guilt issue can get complicated and many grieving teens feel guilty for not having spent more time with the deceased. Grief is a painful, tough subject, and your grandchild may feel shame if some friends abandon her or him to avoid this subject. "Your teenager longs to be popular and envied, not pitied," the authors explain. For this reason, and others, a teenage grandchild may refuse counseling.

Teen grief takes many forms. Here are some from Dyer's list.
- Concentration problems (distracted, forgetful)
- Extreme emotions, such as anger, guilt, and fear
- Self-blame
- Questions about death and mortality
- Sensing the presence of the deceased
- Spending more time with friends
- Masking feelings with humor
- Loneliness, isolation, and changes in self-image
- Depression and possible suicidal thoughts

You can help by being honest, listening, involving your grandchild in plans, encouraging creative projects, and answering questions. Remaining calm will help your grandchild to be calm.

Alan D. Wolfelt, PhD, offers coping tips for teens in his book, *Healing Your Grieving Heart for Teens*. He lists one hundred practical tips and, since there isn't room for all of them here, I chose my favorites.

Do something fun and dedicate it to the one you lost. After Helen died, I came up with the idea of taking a trip to Alaska with the twins. The two-and-a-half-week trip, by cruise and land, was just what we needed. The twins roamed the ship; I think they checked every nook and cranny. We enjoyed the food, the entertainment, and laughed together, something we hadn't done in weeks. I think the trip prepared the twins for living with us after both parents died.

Do something the person who died liked to do. The twins' father loved fishing and they loved it too. They often went boating and fishing on the Mississippi River, a thirty-five-minute drive from Rochester. After his father died, my grandson went fishing on the Mississippi River with some of his friends. He and his friends also camped on some sand dunes along the shore.

Remember the good times. Grief recovery can't be rushed. The time came when we could share stories about Helen. Our granddaughter remembered her mother's awesome meatloaf. I told her it was my recipe. "I know," she replied, "but it wasn't the same." My meatloaf would never be the same, I replied, and that was the truth. Nothing could replace the love and care Helen put into fixing meals for the twins.

Grandparents and grandchildren need to talk about grief, say their loved one's names, and remember them in various ways. Gestault therapist Judy Tatelbaum, author of *The Courage to Grieve*, thinks it's helpful to make good things from grief. "Making our grief meaningful can be the antidote to despair and suffering as well as the stepping-stone to personal growth and achievement," she writes. You'll know the moment when it comes—a feeling of hope you haven't felt in a long time—and the possibility of joy. When you have these feelings you're on the way to choosing happiness.

The Happiness Choice

The US Constitution grants citizens the right to pursue happiness. GRGs have the right to pursue happiness, yet many fail to find it. But happiness isn't a chase; it comes from the inside and is something we create for ourselves. Abraham Lincoln once said, "Most folks are about as happy as they make up their minds to be." I chose happiness for myself, and other grandparents have made the same choice. Early in my grandparenting journey I realized I was blessed. I had a loving husband, loving family, a home, and a career I enjoyed. All of these worked in my favor.

Personality worked in my favor as well. Happiness begins with the decision to view life through a bright lens instead of a dark one.

Tom Valeo writes about the happiness choice in a WebMD website article, "Strategies for Happiness: 7 Steps to Becoming a Happy Person." The first step is to choose happiness. Other steps include gratitude, forgiveness, positive thinking, friendship, and meaningful activities. You may have thought about these steps before but not put them together. I choose happiness by countering negative thoughts with positive ones and have been doing this for years.

In their book *Teen Grief Relief*, Dr. Heidi Horsley and Dr. Gloria Horsley call this technique *thought stopping*. If thought stopping doesn't work, the Horsleys suggest wearing a rubber band on your wrist and snapping it gently when you need to focus your thoughts. I tried this and it works.

Maybe it's time to leave sadness behind and enjoy the happiness you deserve. Happiness comes in drops like rain. The drops accumulate and eventually you have a puddle of happiness, or even a lake. Elizabeth Gilbert, author of *Eat, Pray, Love*, started keeping a "Happiness Jar" many years ago. It's easy to do, according to Gilbert, and takes about thirty-five seconds. She tells how to do it in her article "Let's Talk About Those Happiness Jars, Shall We?" Every day, at the end of the day, she jots down a happy moment on a small piece of paper, dates it, folds the paper, and sticks it in a jar.

Her happiness moments aren't big ones, they're little things: "a bit of sun on my face, a pleasant encounter on the sidewalk . . ."

There aren't any rules, Gilbert continues, and you can do "absolutely whatever you like with it, sweet friends." Gilbert told friends about the idea, friends told their friends, and the idea spread. When I wrote *Help! I'm Raising My Grandkids*, I didn't know about the Happiness Jar idea. I learned about it when I became John's primary caregiver. At first, I kept one Happiness Jar and was faithful about putting papers in it. But caregiving tasks diverted me and I only occasionally put papers in the jar. Then I decided to keep two jars, one for personal happiness and one for caregiving happiness. Following Gilbert's instructions, I started a new jar on the first day of the next year.

The papers became a chronology of John's progress and could be a chronology of your grandchild's progress. The papers document life's little moments, which are really big moments—a child losing the first tooth, learning to jump rope, joining a Scout troop. You have the power to replace shadows of grief with sunlight. Each new day gives you the chance to choose happiness over sadness. You don't have to use a jar. A box or plastic container will also work. If you don't want to fold papers, just drop them in the vessel.

"What's inside is simply—very simply—the best part of our life on earth," Gilbert concludes. So get some papers, find a vessel, and start your Happiness Jar. You may also keep a happiness log on the computer. These tips may help you make the happiness choice.

What Works

1. Understand that all GRGs are grieving for something.

2. Be alert to different types of grief.

3. Watch for anticipatory grief.

4. Remember that your grandchild is grieving too.

5. Check your support system.

6. Learn more about how kids grieve.

7. Help your grandchild to express grief.

8. Find a linking object to comfort your grandchild.

9. Find something to be happy about each day.

10. Keep a Happiness Jar.

CHAPTER 4

Creating a Grandfamily

Facing new challenges doesn't mean you can't enjoy them. Raising a grandchild adds humor, zest, and excitement to your life. Life has given you another time of wonder. Unfortunately, some people miss out on this time. Creating a grandfamily, a blend of two generations, begins with love, and this is the basis of everything you do.

Admittedly, after you've suffered many losses, it can be hard to enjoy anything. Still, it's possible. I remember sitting at the round table in the kitchen with my family after Helen died. One of the twins said something that made me laugh, a welcome surprise. Since I hadn't laughed in a long time, I laughed really hard. "Grandma thought that was funny," my grandson commented. Laughter is contagious, and my laughter made the twins laugh. It also changed the mood at the table. A good laugh relieves tension and makes us feel better. Make laughter part of every day with your grandchild.

There are many things to consider when creating a grand-family: legal papers, basic childcare, household rules, maintaining friendships, education, hobbies, and more. Gathering the documents you need to create a grandfamily isn't a laughing matter; it's serious business. For us, creating a grandfamily began with Helen's will and the county court. We had to hire a lawyer to help us navigate the court system. The lawyer, a friend of Helen's, drew up the will, and knew about her case. Thankfully, Helen appointed us as the twins' guardians in her will. Other grandparents aren't as fortunate. You may be trying to adopt your grandchild now, or involved in a family fight about who has custody of your grandchild.

An AARP article, "Grandfamilies Guide: Getting Started," by Amy Goyer, tells grandparents to gather documents and keep them in a three-ring binder. Goyer thinks you need these documents:

- Birth certificate
- Parents' divorce papers
- Grandchild's Social Security number
- Medical/dental records
- Power of Attorney (POA)
- Guardianship or adoption papers
- Report cards

Other documents, such as citizenship or military papers if a parent is on active duty, may also be necessary. Get at least ten copies of the death certificate if your grandchild's parent has died. Written letters, email printouts, and photos are also things to store in the notebook. After you've gathered legal documents together, it's time to think about the care you provide. Providing basic care may be more time-consuming than you imagined.

Begin with the Basics

A grandchild's basic needs fall into two groups: physical and mental. Physical needs are obvious: nutritious food, a safe place to live, space for physical activity, clean air to breathe, and medical and dental care. Mental needs may be less obvious—learning, praise, problem-solving, and exploring the child's world. Love is the most important need, and you need to assure your grandchild or grandchildren that they are loved. Consistency is also a need, especially for a grandchild who has experienced many life changes. John and I met the twins' physical needs and most of their mental needs. We couldn't provide a lively environment because we had aches and pains that come with aging and weren't sports nuts. I've often joked about marrying John because he wasn't addicted to watching football. He does like to watch golf tournaments and figure skating, however.

We knew we had to be consistent, dependable grandparents, keep our promises, and keep the twins informed. I think we did these things. John and I also told the twins that we weren't trying to replace their parents. Instead, we were acting *as* parents. An older child will understand this. A toddler, preschooler, or grade-school child will not. Your actions will have to demonstrate this concept. Keep your message short and end with an upbeat sentence, such as "Being your grandpa is so much fun."

Johanna Carlson discusses children's needs in a Health Guidance website article, "The Basic Needs of Every Child." She begins by saying that children's basic needs can be complex because they are a product of their environment. Your grandchild may have lived in an unstable home for months, and this experience will stay with her or him for a long time. Failure to meet a grandchild's basic needs can result in physical and emotional harm. Carlson believes that child neglect comes in many forms. Are you meeting your grandchild's needs?

Let's start with nutrition. Preparing food for your grandchild can become a want-versus-need situation. Television ads tout many unhealthy foods—high-sugar cereals and drinks, cookies that masquerade as nutrition bars, and super-salty foods. Read the entire product label before you put anything in your grocery cart. Some manufacturers reduce the serving size to make the nutrition numbers look better. Pay close attention to the serving size, and whether it is realistic for your grandchild. A teenager may eat two or three times the amount stated on the label.

There's an old saying that humans eat with their eyes. Certainly, a colorful meal is more appealing than brown glop. Consider food colors when you plan meals. A young grandchild will be more apt to eat a colorful meal, and one that's served on a small plate.

Children of all ages need a routine and rules to follow. Like girders that support a building, a routine provides structure for the day. Rules make it easier for children to adjust to a new family structure. I typed a list of our household rules and posted it on the refrigerator. I used our last name and the twins' last name for the heading to emphasize the blending of two families.

Hodgson-Welby Household Rules

Change sheets weekly and wash in hot or warm water.

Clean out dryer trap when you're done.

Tell us when you're low on clothing, school supplies, medications, and money.

Empty bathroom waste basket when it's full.

List all appointments/events on master calendar.

Keep us informed of your plans.

Tell us when you're low on snacks.

Fill the car gas tank when the gauge says ¼ full.

Let Grandma know, a day ahead of time, if you need to bring food to an event.

Let Grandma know, several hours ahead of time, if a friend is coming for dinner and/or a sleepover.

No phone calls, loud music, or drum music after 9:00 p.m.

Always remember that we love you and are proud of you.

Rules for young grandchildren may include brushing teeth with or without help, putting toys away, and stashing dirty clothes in the hamper. Try to stick to your household rules and gently respond to lapses. Be willing to tweak your rules if they aren't working. Household rules may have to change, and you need to be willing to make these changes. Your grandchild or grandchildren may have suggestions for household rules.

After they received their driver's licenses the twins stayed out later. Although John and I went to bed, we didn't sleep well because our grandparenting instincts were still active. We would awaken after midnight and ask, "Are the kids home yet?" If one twin was home, we waited anxiously for the other, and the next day we looked and acted like sleep-deprived people.

I recall one sleepless night vividly.

Our grandson had come home, but our granddaughter was still out. I was awake for hours and finally drifted off to sleep. I awakened at 5:30 a.m. and, when I got up, was shocked to see our granddaughter's bedroom door was open, and the bed empty. I couldn't believe my eyes, so I peeked under the covers. Suddenly, my mind went back to the night Helen died, and the equally terrible night the twins' father died. I began to panic. Painful images, colors, and feelings raced through my mind. Was I experiencing PTSD? Had another tragic accident happened?

Just as I was about to call the police, our granddaughter walked in the back door. "Where have you been?" I asked worriedly.

"Oh, we were watching a late-night movie, and I fell asleep on Barb's couch," she replied. I asked our granddaughter why she hadn't called us. "I just woke up a few minutes ago," she said. Her explanation was matter-of-fact; my feelings were not. In fact, my anxiety lasted all morning. Some household rules had been dropped, but this incident created a new one: Keep Grandma and Grandpa informed.

Regular physical activity is a basic need that is often overlooked. Recently I heard that many school systems are dropping recess. I was dismayed to hear this. Too many kids spend their time watching television, using the computer, or using their cell phones. Children need to run and play and laugh outdoors. In safe neighborhoods, park visits and walks can become regular physical activities. Before you head out, make sure you and your grandchild are wearing comfortable shoes and dressed for the weather. Riding bikes may also be a shared activity. The important thing is to keep moving.

More information on basic needs can be found on the Kids Health website. They posted a series of safety checklists that pertain to seven areas of the home: kitchen, child's bedroom, outdoors/backyard/pool, structure (walls, floors, doors, windows), electrical (heating and cooling), bathroom, garage, and laundry area. The lists are long and can't be included here. To read them, visit kidshealth.org and enter the search words *Household Safety Checklists.*

Identify Responsibilities and Tasks

Learning to be a GRG or GAP takes time. Your new role will become clearer to you with practice. My granddaughter's gymnastics banquet is a good example. I knew I was supposed to bring food to share, but my granddaughter forgot to tell me I was also supposed to bring plates, cups, and utensils. Fortunately, another family had brought extras and gave them to us. The next year, I added these supplies to my shopping list.

Every grandparenting responsibility generates its own tasks. Just as roots spread out from a tree, tasks spread out from responsibilities. One responsibility can generate three, four, or more tasks, and they add up to an action-packed day.

I made a diagram of some of my responsibilities and tasks. Although each responsibility leads to three tasks, there are actually more. Having teens in the house created dozens of responsibilities and, consequently, my task list was a long one. This chart gives you a snapshot of my life.

Responsibility: Fix balanced, nutritious meals.

Frequent trips to the grocery store
Making dishes from scratch
Giving grandchildren food choices

Responsibility: Provide a comfortable, cozy home.

Painting bedroom walls
Hiring a moving van to move furniture to our home
Replacing old carpet with wood flooring

Responsibility: Provide and/or arrange for medical and dental care.

Arranging for twins to see our dentist
Using father's medical/dental insurance
Arranging for counseling

Responsibility: Provide transporation.

Taxi service when needed
Loaning my car to the twins
Keeping my car gas tank full

Review your responsibilities and tasks. Can some be delegated to other family members? A relative may be willing to come and babysit for a few hours. Would hiring a part-time nanny be helpful? You don't want to wear yourself out.

Legal Matters

You can't let legal matters wear you out either. If you haven't thought about legal matters, now is the time to do it. You will need legal help if you removed your grandchild from an unsafe home. Nobody wants a custody fight, yet this can happen, and it's painful. You may not know the types of custody that exist. In some instances, grandparents petition the court for custody because the parents are unfit. A grandchild may be put in legal foster care, an arrangement for a grandchild or grandchildren to live with grandparents or other relatives. Adoption is another option. Under this arrangement, parental rights are terminated, and grandparents are legally and financially responsible for a grandchild.

Becoming a guardian or conservator requires substantial paperwork. For example, the county court required written proof of how we spent the twins' inheritance, their Social Security funds, and money in their bank accounts. The purpose of this documentation is to prevent adults from taking money from minors. Our guardianship was rescinded shortly after the twins turned eighteen, yet they still lived at home with us, and we were still involved in their lives. The twins lived with us until they graduated from college. We still think of them as our kids.

Our lawyer guided us through the court process. Going to court for the first time was an emotional experience. Our case was the third on the docket and we listened to the first few cases before ours. One woman started to cry, pulled herself together, and thanked the judge for giving her money to feed her grandchildren. Her story brought tears to my eyes. The second case was equally emotional, and I was crying by the time our case came up. Prepare yourself emotionally if you have to go to court.

You may be unable to fulfill your financial obligations. Help is available from national and state governments. Lyra T. Coffey, in her article "10 Tips for Grandparents Raising Grandchildren," asks grandparents to examine their legal status before seeking help. You may have some thorny questions. Who owns the car that is parked in the parent's garage? Can your grandchild inherit the car? Do the contents of a vacated house belong to your grandchild's parents or your grandchild? A lawyer can help you answer these questions. Legal Aid may also be able to help.

Don't let your grandfamily fall apart because you overlooked a legal step or document. Keep at it for yourself, your grandchild, and the next generation. Your teenage grandchild may ask questions about legal matters, and you should answer them honestly and briefly. Provide details and documentation if your grandchild has more questions. No doubt about it, court matters are serious stuff.

Have Fun and Tell Stories

This may be a stressful time for you, yet you need to make time for fun and enjoy your grandchild. Plan some activities that all family members can enjoy. The activities you choose need to be age-appropriate. Some of our relatives lived in a cabin in the woods, and we visited them several times. Cousins were visiting at the same time and, if the noise level was any indication, the cousins had a great time together. A couple of times the twins brought high school friends with them. They swam in the lake, went out in a boat, fished for sunfish, and walked in the woods.

Having fun with your grandchild can be exploring, a learning activity, or telling stories. Journalist Sally Stich thinks children favor some activities over others, and lists them in her article "8 Activities Kids Love to Do with Grandparents," posted on the Grandparents website. The activities she lists are participating in a scavenger hunt, looking at baby photos, playing card games, baking cookies and eating them, playing video games, getting a back rub, going to the library, and rummaging through a jewelry box.

Simple activities often turn out to be the best, like a summer picnic or telling stories. John and I come from storytelling families. When I was growing up, my family sat on the front porch in the summertime, and we stayed out until dark telling stories and eating ice cream.

Our granddaughter likes to tell the story about her learning to say the word "cute." I don't know how she did it, but she managed to make a four-letter word a four-syllable word.

My stories tend to be brief and include gestures, whereas John's stories are filled with details. One of his stories took so many detours the twins and I could hardly follow it. "Cut to the chase!" I exclaimed. The twins gave each other "the look" and tried not to smile. I'm ashamed of my outburst and should have been more patient with John. Yes, we are guilty of repeating the same stories. The twins always listened patiently and laughed when we hoped they would.

Are you wondering about which stories to share? Journalist Lisa Carpenter offers suggestions in her article "6 Stories to Tell Your Grandchildren Again and Again," published on the *Huffington Post* website. Her suggestions are how you met your partner in grandparenting, the day your grandchild was born, your school memories, the first job you ever had, your favorite job, and the proudest moment of your life. Sharing stories creates positive connections and are part of family history. The experiences you have with your grandchild may become family stories.

One of our family stories stands out from the others.

For some time, John and I wanted to replace the mouse-gray carpet that came with our house. Ugh! Hectic as our lives were, we decided to do something for ourselves and replace the carpet with wood flooring. Eddie, our flooring expert and a true craftsman, laid the wood, hung a plastic barrier from the ceiling, and started varnishing. Even with the plastic barrier, the varnish smell was so strong we decided to go to the movies to escape it. Our grandson went downstairs to watch television.

Eddie was sitting in his truck in front of the driveway when we returned from the movies. He looked worried and pale. "Something's wrong," I said to John, as we pulled alongside the truck. "Hi, Eddie," I began.

"Which do you want first, the good news or the bad?" Eddie asked. I chose the good news. "The good news is I have insurance," he said. "The bad news is that I spilled a can of varnish down your stairs." We went inside to assess the damage. Eddie hadn't spilled a small can of varnish, he spilled an industrial-size can, and the carpeted steps were blotched with it. The newly painted wall was also spotted with varnish. This was going to be one heck of a cleanup job.

"What happened?" I asked. Eddie recounted the story. Apparently our grandson was using his cell phone and accidentally hit the panic button. We had an alarm system and this signal went to police headquarters. Minutes later, a police car pulled up in front of the house and two officers emerged with guns drawn. They rang the front doorbell which, unfortunately, played "There's No Place Like Home," a song so obnoxious it's a wonder the officers didn't shoot the bell. (It came with the house, but programming instructions didn't.) Nobody answered, so the officers entered the house and saw the main floor was a wreck, filled with furniture from upstairs.

Fearing foul play, the officers went upstairs, their guns still drawn, approached Eddie from behind, and scared him out of his wits. "I saw their shadows first," Eddie explained. "I turned around, and saw two police and the guns." After the officers realized nothing was wrong, they went to check the basement. They opened the door just as our grandson reached the top step. He was shocked to see the police.

Everything was straightened out and the officers left. A week later we received a stern letter from the Rochester Police Department that said if this happened again we would be fined $350. Processing Eddie's insurance claim took several weeks. The varnishing job was finished, new carpet was installed, and the wall was repainted. Although it wasn't funny at the time, we laugh about the story now. The "Guns Drawn" story is now part of family lore.

Young children make up stories while they're playing. Stock up on basic play materials if you're caring for a young child. A sandbox, sand toys, wooden building blocks, and water play are some of the best activities for young children. All over the world, children gravitate to these play materials. I was reminded of this as John and I walked along a street in Taipei, Taiwan. Three young children were playing in a sandpile. The sand was from a nearby construction project and the kids couldn't resist it. They picked up sand with their hands and watched it trickle to the ground. Although they tried to mold the sand, it wasn't wet enough, yet they kept trying. Sand seemed to fascinate them.

A middle school or high school grandchild may be a "techie," but this age group enjoys reminders of childhood—a stuffed animal, Frisbee, or puzzle. Be on the lookout for these things because they're great for rainy days, stocking stuffers, and birthday gifts. Take advantage of community resources—craft shows, exhibits, a kite-flying contest, meet-the-author events at the library, children's story hours, children's museums, music in the park, visiting the fire station, and neighborhood night out. Try to have fun each day.

What can you do for fun? What does your grandchild like to do? These shared activities may bring family members together. We did many of these things with the twins.

- Visit a science museum.
- Spend the weekend in a cabin.
- Have lunch at an ethnic restaurant or food truck.
- Watch a parade.
- Go to a street fair.
- Order take-out food.
- Play Frisbee or catch.
- Take the dog (if you have one) for a walk.
- Watch sailboats on the lake.
- See the latest movie in town.
- Rake leaves together.
- Put up holiday decorations.
- Ride bikes. Your town may have bike trails.

Other activity ideas will be in the newspaper (print or online version) and in television ads. Check with your grandchild before you make plans. An activity that interests you may not interest her or him. Plan activities well ahead and note them on the calendar. Your grandchild, depending on age, may have some suggestions for shared activities. Involving your grandchild helps to make the event go well.

Plan Parent Visits

A troubled adult child, the parent of your grandchild, may still want to stay in contact with their child. Your grandchild may look forward to this visit or feel nervous; you may be nervous too. Diane Bales, an extension human development specialist, shares some ideas for parent visits in a University of Georgia website article, "Grandparents Raising Grandchildren: Helping a Grandchild Stay in Contact with Parents." These tips will help parental visits go smoothly.

Be flexible with schedules. Your plans may change and the parent's plans may change. When you're planning, it's a good idea to make a contingency plan. Try to have visits on a certain day of the week at a certain time. List visits on the calendar. Put stickers on these dates so a young grandchild can keep track of them.

Treat the parent or parents respectfully. Despite past arguments, keep your feelings under control. Be courteous and, if possible, let the parent or parents do most of the talking. You may wish to end the visit with a funny story about your grandchild. Ending a visit with laughter sets the stage for future visits.

Keep communication lines open. Visits can be stressful and you may wish to make a list of talking points and practice them beforehand. Because a high voice can indicate stress, keep your voice low and calm. Talk about your grandchild's school achievements and new friends. Share any new contact information you may have, such as a new email address or cell phone number.

Respect your grandchild's feelings. Parent visits can arouse conflicting feelings—happiness at seeing a parent, sadness when your grandchild recalls sad memories. "Don't make children feel guilty about enjoying the time they spent with their parent," Bales advises. Although you may not feel it, try to act happy about each visit.

Strive for normal. You know life isn't normal, but you can make visits seem that way. Offer the parent or parents a snack. Share news, things like a grandson learning to ride a two-wheeler or a granddaughter's new haircut. Playing a game together may foster normalcy. A parent may also read a story to your grandchild.

Be consistent. Share your house rules with the parent or parents before visits. According to Bales, grandparents should expect some deviation from rules during the first visits. If this happens, remind the parent or parents that rules come from your safety and well-being concerns. Everyone is finding their way, and this is a time for patience.

Watch for signs of stress. Before or during the visit, your grandchild may complain of a stomachache, headache, or muscle aches. Your grandchild may start to argue. Keep your cool, and reassure your grandchild with a hug and calming activity. Baking cookies together is an activity everyone can enjoy.

Give your grandchild some control. Ask your grandchild to suggest activities for the visit. You may plan things to talk about, school work to complete, or a new hobby to try. Let your grandchild gather items for the visit: a board game, favorite books, a football, or craft supplies. She or he may also plan what to wear.

Sadly, some parents are a no-show. The only thing you can do is tell your grandchild the truth in age-appropriate words. You may talk about future visits, but don't build them up too much. A parent may be unable to visit because she or he is in the hospital or undergoing drug treatment. To stay in touch, your grandchild may send the parent letters, drawings, and photos. According to

Bales, it's a good idea to listen attentively to your grandchild, and let them know she or he is loved.

I think it's important to say, "I love you" and say it often. These tips will help you create a grandfamily.

What Works

1. Gather important documents together and store in a three-ring binder.

2. Get legal assistance if you think you need it.

3. Provide for your grandchild's physical and mental needs.

4. Compile a list of household rules and display it.

5. Make regular physical activity part of your care.

6. Identify responsibilities and the tasks they create.

7. Make your own responsibilities and tasks chart.

8. Choose activities the whole family can enjoy.

9. Have fun with your grandchild and tell stories.

10. Plan for parental visits and, depending on age, involve your grandchild in plans.

Helen, holding the Manx flag, John, and the eight-year old twins on the Isle of Man.

The twins at their high school graduation in 2009. They both graduated with honors.
Photo courtesy of Ken Presley.

John and twins in Alaska in the summer of 2007. They are standing
next to the Alaska pipeline.

My granddaughter with her soon-to-be fiancé. This photo was taken at her Coe College art installation in 2013.

John looking dapper in his wheelchair just before escorting our granddaughter down the aisle on her wedding day in 2014.

Our grandson with his girlfriend in front of the Mayo banner on his first day at The Mayo Clinic School of Medicine in 2017. He will be the third physician in our immediate family.

Family portrait taken on Dec. 23, 2017 at our home in Rochester, MN.
Wonderful food, wonderful evening.

CHAPTER 5

Communicating with Grandkids

Good communication is key to creating a grandfamily. Complex as communication can be, the definition is simple—imparting or exchanging information or news. Whatever the information or news may be, your goal is to make sure your grandchild gets the message. You may think you accomplished this goal only to find out your grandchild didn't pay attention or recall what you said. How can you improve communication?

John and I felt like we were on a communication team, and the twins were the other members. I can't speak for the twins, but I think they wanted good communication as much as we did. None of us ever used the attack approach. There was no yelling, screaming, or threatening at our house. Instead, we spoke calmly and respectfully. Courtesy and kindness foster good communication. Word choices affect communication as well.

As you might expect, the twins were stressed when they moved in with us. We were all grieving. At the time, we were trying to find our way, and sometimes we spoke sharply. My granddaughter said something to her brother in a sharp voice—too terse for me. I didn't think her word choices were the best either. "You're an honors English student," I said. "Could you rephrase that sentence?" She grinned at me and revised her sentence and the tone of her voice. Our granddaughter was willing to do this, and I respected her for it.

Be careful about your word choices when talking with your grandchild. Your word choices need to be age-appropriate. Frustrated as you may be, avoid attack words because they impede or halt communication. In her article "Communication Is Important for Grandparents Raising Grandchildren," Cheri Burcham, a family life educator, asks parents to resist these kinds of words. Attack words escalate emotions, according to Burcham, and make the other person—your precious grandchild—feel unsafe. They also make your grandchild afraid to say what she or he wants to say.

From your grandchild's perspective, life is all mixed up, and consistency helps her or him to figure things out. No matter what their age, consistency makes children feel safe. In fact, the lack of consistency makes children feel insecure, or "even chaotic," according to Dr. Bonnie Zucker, author of the article "Parents are Asking Why Consistency is Important" posted on the University of Illinois website. She believes that consistent communication helps grandchildren develop self-confidence.

When communication is consistent, your grandchild knows what to do and what is expected. So put consistency on your communications tips list next to a positive attitude and a modulated voice.

Your Voice

The way you use your voice can change your message. Ending a sentence on a high pitch turns every sentence into a question. Pitch can also be an indication of emotion. A high voice can signal fear or worry, and your grandchild will notice this immediately. Try to use a calm voice if you're upset. In fact, a calm voice can be more powerful than a loud one. Remember, your grandchild is your audience.

Deep inside, a teenage grandchild may be thinking, *I'm so glad Grandma (or Grandpa) isn't shouting at me. I've heard too much shouting already.* A younger grandchild may be thinking, *Grandpa's loud voice scares me.* Babies are smart, and an infant can pick up on your stress. Using a harsh, loud voice can frighten an infant grandchild and, in response, she or he may start wailing. However, a soothing voice can calm a fussy baby.

During my first year of teaching I learned the power of a calm voice. Actually, it was the power of a whisper. In the winter I caught a terrible cold and developed laryngitis. Long after the cold was gone, I was still unable to speak normally. Since I wasn't contagious anymore and had used all of my sick leave, I returned to teaching. I thought my fragile voice would create a chaotic classroom. It didn't. My eighty kindergarten students, forty in the morning and forty in the afternoon—a staggering total that is illegal today—were fascinated by my whispers. They were so fascinated they whispered back, and the room became quieter and quieter.

I had the quietest classroom in the school. The whispering experiment taught me that you don't need to speak loudly to be understood.

Is your voice loud or soft? Is your voice clear or muffled? Toastmasters International created a booklet about voice and diction titled "Your Speaking Voice." These tips may help you communicate with your grandchild. You may wish to record your voice to hear it better. Try to be objective and determine if you're using your voice properly. Vocal variety adds interest, according to Toastmasters, and a good speaker may use twenty-five pitches to get their points across.

Toastmasters asks members to determine the kind of voice they have and lists four types in its booklet. I've added comments.

Do you have a quiet or booming voice? Your grandchild may flinch from hearing a loud voice, so it's wise to modulate your voice. You can also emphasize certain words, such as *love, good,* and *happy.*

Do you have a monotonous or interesting voice? Speaking in a monotonous voice puts a grandchild to sleep. You may almost put yourself to sleep. In contrast, a melodious voice will keep your grandchild interested in what you're saying. Your message will be received.

Does your voice convey emotion? According to Toastmasters, a good speaking voice expresses emotional color. I think honesty affects emotional color and always tried to be honest with the twins.

Do you mumble or enunciate? Speak clearly and continue to support your voice with breath until you reach the end of the sentence. Learning diaphragmatic breathing can help you do this. You can see videos of this technique on the Internet.

Your grandchild may not understand you if you lower the volume of your voice at the end of a sentence. This can be an unconscious habit. Practice key messages aloud before you share them with your grandchild.

Keep Sentences Short

Long, rambling sentences can be ineffective and, while you're talking, your grandchild may stop listening. Robert Bolton, PhD, author of *People Skills: How to Assert Yourself, Listen to Others, and Resolve Conflicts,* calls this an "interpersonal gap." The next time you talk with your grandchild, think about sentence structure. Conversations with long sentences may have a sender but no receiver. In other words, you're talking to yourself. Are you rambling or are your sentences to the point?

Long sentences fail for several reasons according to the article "Power of Short Sentences," posted on the Cute Writing blog. The first reason is the writer's or speaker's ego—in this instance, your ego. You may want to show off your language skills or intelligence. This can be a conscious or unconscious act. Lack of vocabulary is another reason for long sentences. Since you can't retrieve the words you seek, you may talk around a topic. By the time you get to the end of the sentence, your grandchild has forgotten the beginning.

Compliments are often delivered in short sentences. Everyone appreciates a compliment, even an infant grandchild who has no words of their own yet. An infant grandchild can sense your compliment. An article on the Family Education website, "Perfecting the Art of the Compliment," offers ideas on this communication skill. The basics of a compliment are sincerity, specificity, unqualified, and without comparison. A comparison can totally ruin a compliment. For example, "You did pretty well on today's test, but better on last week's test." Who needs a half-hearted compliment like this? Make sure your compliment is *really* a compliment.

I complimented my granddaughter on her new haircut and the color of the sweater she was wearing. My one-sentence compliments made her smile. I complimented my grandson on his helpfulness and he looked pleased. Resist the urge to supply too many details, which can almost erase a compliment. One-sentence compliments are remembered and savored. The twins often complimented me on my cooking, and that made me feel good.

"How to Give and Receive Compliments," an article by Chirantan Basu, offers three tips. I changed the wording to "be" statements and added comments.

Be genuine. You don't want your compliment to come across as smarmy. After you've complimented your grandchild, it's best to leave it alone.

Be specific. "You did a good job of putting your toys away" is a specific compliment. You may compliment an older child on his or her kindness or a striking photo.

Be appropriate. Pick a good time and place. Finding time to compliment teens can be a challenge because they're so busy with school, activities, and friends. Instead of a verbal compliment, give your grandchild a written one. Write a one-sentence compliment on a sticky note and put it on their door.

As short as a sentence is, you can still include the reason for it. My grandson and I were going to the store, and I let him drive my car for practice. It was winter and the streets were covered with snow. The weather bureau warned about black ice, which is hard to see and dangerous. I was concerned. "I don't think you're leaving a large enough margin of safety for road conditions," I said. "And I think you're driving too fast." He slowed down.

You may have to edit sentences before you say them. Natalie Pond and Hanna Jensen give five examples of editing in their article "Revising for Clarity," posted on the Center for Writing and Speaking blog. Although their tips are for written sentences, they are also helpful for spoken ones.

Get rid of non-essential words. This includes words with the same or similar meaning. I think GRGs need to avoid the word *always*, as with the comment, "Your room is always messy." This may not be accurate.

Use simpler construction is another tip. Your grandchild doesn't want to hear a long introduction or endless details. Just get to the point.

Don't keep repeating. I'm guilty of this and used to repeat sentences because I thought the person wasn't listening. Repetition can be annoying, so I stopped doing this.

Use the best words, not the most. I love this tip! Short words, such as *love*, are powerful and can have deep meaning.

Finally, sympathize with your grandchild. A little sympathy can win your grandchild to your side and control feelings that are starting to get out of control.

Be an Active Listener

You need to listen to your grandchild and listen carefully. To be an active listener, give your grandchild your total attention. Active listening takes more energy than passive listening and is the most powerful tool in your grandparenting tool belt. According to the article "The Skill of Listening" posted on the Center for Parenting Education website, listening is the best way to create a caring relationship. Listening shows how much you care. There are four steps to follow in order to practice active listening.

1. Stop what you're doing and pay attention to your grandchild.

2. Look directly at your grandchild.

3. Pay close attention to what she or he is saying.

4. Show you understand by nodding your head or making a brief reply.

These steps sound simple, but the Center for Parent Education says active listening is a sophisticated skill that takes years to master. Parents (and grandparents) need to develop some attitudes for active listening to be successful. Be prepared to accept your grandchild's feelings and separate your feelings from her or his feelings. Remember that feelings can change quickly.

Mentally reversing roles can be helpful. How would you feel if you were your grandchild? When I reversed roles in my mind, I thought of my high school years, how vulnerable I felt inside, and my desire to achieve. At the time, Great Neck High School on Long Island, New York, was one of the top in the nation. Eighty percent of the graduates went to college, a high percentage then. The competition was stiff, and I felt like a goldfish in the sea. Your grandchild may feel the same way and not know which way to "swim."

While you're honing your active listening skills, listen for signal words. Our grandson asked if he could sleep under a bridge with his buddies. I'm originally from Long Island, where anyone who sleeps under a bridge is homeless, running from the law, or involved with drugs. We met with the mother of one of our grandson's buddies. She knew the sheriff, who happened to be a woman, and called her. It was safe to sleep under the bridge mid-week, according to the sheriff, but not on weekends because of vagrants.

"I'll be glad to check on them," the sheriff offered. We decided to check the site and all of us went there. The sleeping area by the river had been cleared. Wood had been gathered and piled for future use. After some deliberation, we let our grandson sleep under the bridge. It was so much fun he wanted to do it again several months later.

"We're supposed to have a hard freeze tonight," I cautioned. "I don't think sleeping under the bridge is a good idea."

"We probably won't do it," my grandson replied. A short while later, he left the house and said he was going to hang out with friends. At 11:45 p.m. the phone rang. It was a police officer. "I'm under the Zumbro River Bridge with another officer," he announced. "Does the name [my grandson's name] mean anything to you?"

"That's my grandson," I replied, "and I asked him not to sleep under the bridge tonight."

"Well, we'll talk to the boys," the officer concluded and hung up. After this incident, I began listening for the word *probably* in conversation. It could mean yes, no, or undecided. For me, *probably* was a signal word that put me on guard.

Listening is more than hearing. Bolton defines listening as a combination of hearing what the other person is saying and suspenseful waiting—"an intense psychological involvement with the other." If you're like me, you've had a conversation with someone who wasn't really listening. True listening requires many skills, according to Bolton: psychological involvement, mirroring what the speaker says, paraphrasing sentences, talking about feelings, and listening for words that describe feelings. Examples of feeling words include *funny, nervous, sad, cool, sweet, ditzy, like, friend, disorganized, organized,* and *supportive.*

Use Three-Part Assertions

Three-part assertions are a handy thing to have in your GRG tool kit. Learning to frame three-part assertions takes practice. The more you practice, the better your assertions will be. Three-part assertions can improve family communication, and the best thing about them is that they work.

Sooner or later, the time comes when you have to be assertive. This can be a challenge because you don't want to hurt your grandchild or cause an argument. Knowing how to frame three-part assertions can keep your grandchild safe. According to Bolton, the parts of an assertion are Behavior + Feelings + Affects = Assertion.

Bolton gives an example of an assertion: "When you don't clean the counter after making snacks, I feel annoyed because it makes more work for me." Below are some examples of three-part assertions. Following Bolton's example, each one begins with the word *when.*

When you don't finish your laundry, I'm frustrated because I can't do mine, and this puts me behind.

When I got in the car today, I was upset to see the gas tank almost empty, and I had to stop for gas.

When you park your car on the street too long, I worry about it getting towed away and having to pay a hefty fine.

When you didn't tell us about school conferences, it looked like we didn't care, and Grandpa and I were embarrassed.

Strive for a matter-of-fact tone when speaking three-part assertions. This technique clarifies ideas and feelings. However, I don't think the technique works with a toddler or younger grandchild. The technique is a good fit for preteens and teenagers. A preteen or teenage grandchild can also use three-part assertions when talking with you. Over time, these assertions may spotlight issues you need to work on together.

Reading Aloud and Communication

Reading to your grandchild gives them words and ideas to communicate. Personally, I think reading aloud has a lifelong impact on communication and promotes literacy. John and I read to our daughters when they were young, and they remembered the stories. My surviving daughter can cite her childhood favorites by title. What does reading aloud do for your grandchild?

An infant grandchild hears the sound of your voice, senses your feelings, and starts to learn words. A toddler grandchild will be fascinated by stories and want you to read them over and over again. A grade school grandchild will listen to you read the story, and then want to read it by herself or himself. A middle school grandchild will enjoy listening to you read aloud. A high school grandchild may want to read to you. In many assisted living facilities and nursing homes, reading aloud is a planned activity.

The benefits of reading aloud are listed in a Six Wise website article, "Reading Aloud to Kids: The 12 Benefits of Reading Out Loud to Children of All Ages." Reading aloud generates an interest in books, illustrations, and reading in general. According to the article, children who are read to become better readers, and do better in school. Your grandchild's vocabulary will expand. A short attention span may become a long attention span thanks to hearing stories. At the end of the story, you have a chance to discuss the book and its ending. What did you think of the pictures? Did you like the ending? How would you have written it? I think the best thing about reading to a young grandchild is the chance to snuggle and feel close.

Most public libraries have story hours for children. The Rochester Public Library has an impressive array of story times for babies, toddlers, preschoolers, and families. Some libraries have story hours for little ones just before bed, and the kids come in their pajamas.

The children's librarian at your public library will be glad to recommend books to you. You can find more recommendations on the Internet, and these articles may help you:

- "The Best Children's Books of All Time" on the *Time* magazine website
- "100 Best Books for Children" on the Teachers First website
- "100 Greatest Books for Kids" on the Scholastic website
- "Best Kids Board Books" on Amazon's website
- "The Ultimate Backseat Bookshelf" on the NPR website
- "Best Books for 10-Year Olds" on the Imagination Soup website.

There's one more aspect of communication to consider—silence. Yes, silence is a form of communication. Kurt Smith, PsyD, LMFT, LLPC, AFC, talks about its power in a PsychCentral website article, "Silence: The Secret Communication." Silence can speak louder than words, Smith notes, and helps us "reach resolution faster." He also says silence can be misused to express anger or punish someone, things you don't want to do. Using silence to communicate takes courage, and that's not always easy to do, Smith concludes.

Silence can be an important grandparenting technique. For example, if your two-year-old grandchild has a tantrum, you can ignore it, remain silent, and go about your business. This reminds me of the time Helen had a tantrum in a department store. It was a whopper, and I didn't comment about it. Instead, I continued to look at merchandise. The sales associate, however, reached behind the counter and was about to give Helen some candy. "Please don't give her that," I said. "It doesn't make sense to reward her for this behavior." The sales associate looked astonished and annoyed at the same time.

Teenagers can say things they don't mean and regret their outbursts later. Your grandchild may say she or he hates you, for example. You have the right to be silent and wait for a suitable, unhurried time to discuss this statement. Several days later, when things have calmed down, you can say the comment was hurtful and explain why. Two words to include in your explanation are *safe* ("I want to keep you safe") and *love,* as with "I love you all the time."

All of these ideas—silence, reading aloud, three-part assertions, active listening, short sentences, an effective voice, and a positive attitude—can improve grandfamily communication. Your grandchild will receive your messages and you will receive theirs.

What Works

1. Approach communication with a positive attitude.

2. Evaluate your voice.

3. Monitor your pitch and tone.

4. When you speak, use short sentences.

5. Be an active listener.

6. Listen for signal words.

7. Use three-part assertions.

8. Encourage your grandchild to use three-part assertions too.

9. Read aloud to your grandchild.

10. Communicate with silence when appropriate.

CHAPTER 6

Grandkids and Learning

Going to school is more than learning; it provides structure and continuity for your grandchild's life. While your grandchild is adjusting to a new home, make sure she or he doesn't get behind in schoolwork. Albert Einstein was a talented genius, and I've always appreciated his outlook on education: "Everything must be made as simple as possible but not one bit simpler." Although you hope your grandchild's education is as simple as possible, you may run into some snags.

We ran into a huge snag—the possibility of the twins being forced to change high schools. When they moved in with us they were in the same school district but another area, and consequently, they were supposed to attend a different high school. But the twins wanted to stay at the same high school, so I went to the school office.

I introduced myself and stated the purpose of my visit. "My grandchildren want to stay in this school," I explained. A secretary nodded, handed me a form, and asked me to sign it. I read every form before I sign it and was shocked at the provisions of this form. The twins couldn't participate in anything—band concerts, choir concerts, sports events, or plays.

"What?" I screamed. Everyone in the office stopped what they were doing and stared at me. The principal came out of his office and asked if he could help. "My grandchildren have lost their mother, their father, their dog, their neighborhood, and they're not going to lose their school," I declared. The office staff continued to stare at me. Apparently the principal knew our story because he was calm and understanding.

"Don't worry, I'll take care of it," he soothed. Months later I learned the reason for the document I didn't sign. Apparently students in the district were changing schools to be on winning teams, an idea that never crossed my mind. The purpose of the form was to prevent these kinds of transfers. Just as the principal promised, he took care of things, and the twins were allowed to continue attending the school they loved.

School Connections

School systems around the world are involving grandparents in school activities. These school districts realize grandparents are a reliable, untapped resource. Dr. Salman Al-Azami and Ian Gyllenspetz cite some activities for grandparents in their booklet "Grandparents and Grandchildren Learning Together," published by the Basic Skills Agency in London, England. Grandparents are going to schools and playing instruments, teaching computer skills, telling stories, reading at story hours, helping with sports, and staffing fair booths.

Getting grandparents involved benefits both generations, according to the authors, and this has an impact on the community. Children benefit because of the bond between grandparents and grandchildren. Schools benefit from the expanded knowledge base. According to the authors, children who attend schools that involve grandparents have better English and math scores. That's good for kids and good for us. Instead of feeling like we have been cast aside, we feel recognized and valued.

When Helen and the twins lived in Monticello, Minnesota, I attended Grandparents' Day at their elementary school. As I approached the door, I saw chalk words on the sidewalk. My granddaughter had written a message in capital letters that read:

WELCOME FAMOUS AUTHOR HARRIET HODGSON!

She had written these words again and again leading up to the entrance of the school. I burst out laughing. Although I'm not a famous author, she thought I was, and that made me tingle from head to toe. Clearly, my granddaughter had put lots of effort into welcoming me.

Connecting with your grandchild's school is voluntary. Working grandparents may not have the time to volunteer at school. After losing four family members in nine months, John and I felt so beleaguered we couldn't volunteer for anything. However, we could attend meetings, school events, and donate money. We loved the choir concerts and band concerts. One of our granddaughter's friends was in a musical. We bought tickets for the musical and enjoyed it immensely. Attending was a way to support our granddaughter's friend and the school.

Your grandchild's school may not have taken advantage of GRGs yet. Call the school and offer to do some of these things:

- Read to young children.
- Tutor a student in English or math.
- Serve as a lunchroom helper.
- Plant a vegetable garden with student help and maintain it.
- Share your talents: play the piano, teach drawing, etc. (I've spoken to elementary students about writing.)
- Give a talk about your occupation.

- Share facts and customs from your native country.

- Work at school fairs and sports events.

- Translate notices and newspapers into another language.

- Collect donated books for the library.

- Help to straighten messy storerooms.

- Donate food for a bake sale.

- Manage a fund-raiser.

- Serve on a party or graduation committee.

Barriers You May Encounter

Despite your knowledge and talents, and the willingness to share them, you may hit some barriers as you help your grandchildren learn. Many of these barriers can be overcome, but some cannot. Still, doing some research and putting effort into overcoming them is worth your time.

Grief was a partial barrier for John and me. To be honest, I don't remember much about 2007, or "the year of death" as we call it. I have fragmented memories, however, and during a conversation with my grandson I recounted one story. "I don't remember it," he admitted. "I don't remember much about that year." I understood what he was saying, for I hardly remembered the year myself, and I told him that. Grief had jammed my memory.

Language is a barrier for many grandparents and keeps them from attending school events or understanding them. A report, "Involving Immigrant and Refugee Families in Their Children's Schools: Barriers, Challenges, and Successful Strategies," funded by a US Department of Education grant, details some of the language barriers. Lack of bilingual staff in schools is one barrier;

school materials printed in English and not translated is another.

You may also face cultural barriers. Where you are from, schools may act independently, and families don't get involved. Schools and teachers are trusted to do their jobs, and parents and grandparents aren't expected to take a role in children's experiences, according to the report. This kind of arrangement may have existed for years, but it could change. I think the growing budget problems and staff shortages will remove this cultural barrier. At least I hope so, because everyone benefits when GRGs and GAPs get involved.

Isolation is another barrier. It may be due to your health problems, neighborhood, or lack of transportation, including public transportation. There may be no bus service to the school. Even if there is service, you may not have time to wait for a bus.

Financial problems can be a huge barrier. When I attended Great Neck High School, the school district paid for notebook paper, something that's unheard of today. If my memory is correct, there were no extra costs for participating in sports. Things have changed. Today, parents and grandparents pay for school supplies, and they cost a lot, especially if the family has several children.

Glenda Phillips Reynolds and her colleagues discuss the school supply barrier in their article "The Role of Grandparents in Educating Today's Children" posted on the *Journal of Instructional Psychology* website. Many grandparents dip into savings to pay for school supplies, Reynolds notes, and this can make grandparents feel disappointed and angry. "The children may feel abandoned even if they are grateful to grandparents," the authors explain. This is hard for children and grandparents alike.

Some school districts conduct donation drives for school supplies. The local television station may also conduct a drive. Watch newspaper and television announcements for information about these drives in case you want to contribute to them or use them as a resource.

Infants and Preschoolers

Early learning sets the tone for future learning. Infant learning begins with pointing at objects, "babble" conversation, learning words, and looking at board books. One of the first books I read to my daughters, *A Boy, a Dog, and a Frog* by Mercer Mayer, had no words at all. The sepia illustrations told a hilarious story. While I turned the pages, the kids provided the dialogue, a process called *picture reading*. We laughed together every time we turned a page. By the way, this book is still in print.

Your grandchild may be a preschooler, and you want her or him to have learning and social experiences. Nursery school may be just the solution. Answer these questions before you enroll your grandchild. The questions come from my teaching experience.

1. Is the preschool accredited by the state?

2. Are the teachers licensed?

3. What is the teacher-student ratio? In Minnesota, it is one teacher per ten children.

4. Is there enough space for the children? This is also a state requirement.

5. Do the children have free access to art materials, books, games, and toys?

6. Does the school have physical activity each day?

7. Is there enough physical activity equipment? The school I taught at had bikes, snow shovels, sand pails, sleds, balls, and other equipment.

8. Are the snacks healthy?

9. Are there enough bathrooms and are they clean?

10. Can parents visit at any time?

11. Are scholarship funds available? My school had scholarships, but I never knew which students received them.

12. Does the school have a good reputation?

Some of these questions may also be applied to middle school and high school students. Talk with parents who have children in the school. Ask about the school's reputation, the quality of the teachers, and after-school activities. Is their child happy at school? Finally, ask the parent if they think their child is getting an education that prepares them for life.

Helping with Homework

At a time you thought homework was behind you, the homework challenge has returned. You may think you need more education if your grandchild asks you to help with homework. What your grandchild is learning in school is much different from when you were learning at that age.

Michele Borba, EdD, examines the homework issue in a Parenting Bookmark website article, "Hot Homework Tips for Parents." Adults, and grandparents like us, need to realize we are helpers, not doers, Borba explains. Sometimes parents (and grandparents) can get carried away and provide too much help. A child's homework project turns into an adult project. According to Borba, the child's effort, not just the end product, should be praised. Doing homework helps your grandchild learn the values of hard work and persistence.

Helping with homework gave me a chance to know the twins better. I didn't help much, however. The twins asked me to proofread some English papers they had written. While I agreed to their request, I told them I would look for errors only and not try to change their writing style.

I did find some typos and a few missing sentences, and the twins were grateful.

Children approach homework differently. Your grandchild may prefer to do homework right after school. Other kids like to take a break and do homework after dinner. Homework is easier when children do it at the same time each day, and in the same place. The twins had their own desks and computers, but they didn't have their own printers. We had an in-house computer network, and the printer was in my office downstairs. While I was writing, I would often be startled by the printer belching out prose. It was good prose too! Every time the twins came to get their printouts, they saw me working.

The US government posted homework ideas on its website. One article, "Homework Tips for Parents," may help GRGs and GAPs. It divides homework into three categories: practice, preparation, and extension. Problems may arise when parents (or grandparents) use techniques that differ from the school's techniques, the article cautions. Thank goodness the twins never asked me to help with math homework, because I wouldn't have been able to do it. Math and I aren't friends.

You can help your grandchild with homework by being positive, having paper, pencils, and report folders on hand, and providing guidance. However, the article also says if a child (or grandchild) is supposed to do an assignment alone, an adult shouldn't interfere. Although your grandchild may be willing to do their homework, she or he may have difficulty fitting it into a busy day. This is where you come in. Give your grandchild a healthy snack before starting homework. Make sure your grandchild has a comfortable place to work and good lighting. Be sure to reduce any background noise.

You can also provide homework help through your local library. In recent years, public libraries have changed drastically, and many have homework help lines. Phone tutoring services may also be available. Libraries have computers for the public to use. Some have computers in student study rooms. If your public library doesn't have these services, or you can't get to the library, a retired teacher may be willing to tutor your grandchild at home. If you notice your grandchild is struggling even with this added help, vision and hearing checks may be warranted. Your grandchild may also need help from a reading specialist.

Thinking about homework made me remember the desk in Helen's living room. The desk was really a dressing table that belonged to my mother. Helen stripped off the varnish, sanded the desk, and painted it white. While we were clearing out her house, a process that took us more than a year, we asked the twins for permission to donate the desk to Goodwill. They agreed. A few days later, one of our granddaughter's friends told her about the desk she purchased from the Goodwill store. The desk was perfect for her college dorm, the friend said, and her description fit Helen's desk. The student loved the desk and we loved the story. My mother's desk had found a new home.

At the end of a busy school day, many students participate in after-school activities. Your grandchild may want to do this. These activities give your grandchild time to be with friends, make new friends, and learn new skills. Girl Scouts and gymnastics were our granddaughter's activities. Our grandson was involved in track, marching band, Scrabble club, and Explorer Scouts for a while.

Both of them were inducted into the National Honor Society and did service projects as part of their membership.

You may be swamped right now, and the thought of after-school activities seems like too much. Don't make a hasty decision, for kids who participate in these activities do better in school, are safer, and are less likely to get into trouble, according to "Why Are Afterschool Programs Good for School-Age Children and Youth?" The article, posted on the Concept to Classroom website, lists the benefits of after-school activities: better reading skills, improved attendance, better quality homework, and high hopes for the future.

The public school system in your city or town may have part-time paid staff to supervise after-school activities, rely on volunteers, or do both. I think after-school activities build self-confidence and give kids a chance to try things out. In future years, your grandchild's after-school activity, such as tennis, may be a permanent activity.

Parent Conferences: Should You Go?

You may have asked yourself this question and the answer is affirmative. Do this for the sake of your grandchild and yourself. Parent-teacher conferences are a way to assess your grandchild's progress. More importantly, the conferences give you a chance to work with teachers. The first year the twins lived with us we missed the conferences because we were overcome with grief. John and I felt bad and vowed to go the next year. We missed parent-teacher conferences again because we learned about them too late.

"When are parent-teacher conferences?" I asked.

"Oh, they were last week," my grandson replied casually.

"We never heard about them," I countered.

Our granddaughter joined the conversation. "Conferences are for parents of kids who are having trouble and getting bad grades," she explained. "We're not."

"Parents' night is crowded," the twins continued, "and you would have had to wait in long lines to speak with teachers." These statements were partly true. I knew the conferences weren't just for parents whose children are doing poorly. But I suspected the kids didn't want us to attend the conferences because we weren't their parents.

I hope you find time to attend parent-teacher conferences. Grandchildren do better when parents and kids work together. Another plus is that you will be an informed grandparent. The first conference can be the beginning of a long relationship with the teacher, and this benefits your grandchild. Your attendance shows that you're interested in your grandchild's work, school activities, and learning in general. School activities include field trips and, in some instances, travel.

The twins' high school planned a science trip to Chicago, and both of them wanted to go. We were all for it. Chicago is an exciting city, and the trip seemed to be well-planned. The trip was a success, and the twins talked about it for several days. My grandson played the trumpet, and the marching band went to Disney World in Orlando, Florida. "We marched down Main Street and everyone was applauding," he recalled. "It was really hot and we were wearing wool uniforms, but it was still fun." Before your grandchild goes on a school trip, you will need to sign permission papers. Make sure your grandchild has enough money, snacks, medications if she or he takes them, and health insurance information.

Grandparents as Life Teachers

You may feel insecure in your GRG or GAP role, but age and experience are on your side. What's more, age and experience really count. There are many things you can teach your grandchild—housekeeping skills, social skills, family history, and skills associated with your talents.

Early childhood education instructor Susan Baxter discusses the impact of grandparents in her article "Grandparents as Teachers" posted on the A Place of Our Own website. To begin with, grandparents have an emotional investment in their grandchildren. "Grandparents already know of the routine, rhythm, and ways to comfort a child," she writes.

The knowledge you share will stay with your grandchild all through life. Knowing how to cook, clean, do laundry, manage money, develop woodworking skills, or produce art prepares your grandchild for the future. The twins were amazed at how many of their college friends didn't know how to do laundry. Friends didn't know how to sort laundry, fold laundry, or care for their clothes. Both of the twins were glad Helen taught them Laundry 101.

You may have special housekeeping tips that will help your grandchild, such as how to fold contour sheets. If you know how to change a tire or repair an engine, share these skills with your grandchild.

Family history is something else to teach your grandchild. As your grandchild matures, she or he will be more curious about family history and want to know about their heritage. The Hodgson family is from the Isle of Man, an island in the middle of the Irish Sea. The Manx people, as they are called, say they can see six kingdoms from the highest peak—the Isle, England, Ireland,

Scotland, Wales, and the Kingdom of God. When the twins were eight years old we took them and our two daughters to the Isle of Man. Our trip began in London. We stayed there for several days and visited Windsor Castle.

"When is the queen coming to see us?" our granddaughter asked. I told her the queen wasn't coming, and our granddaughter became angry.

"I want to see the queen!" she demanded. She doesn't remember this, but the photo of her standing with her mother and brother are in the memory books I made for them.

Grandparents who are raising their grandchildren are keepers of history. Look at family photos with your grandchild. Check with family members if some photos are puzzling. Relatives may be able to identify the people in the photos. You may also make a scrapbook about your family and its history. John and I hope our family history, and the life skills we taught the twins, will help them in later years. We also hope the twins see us as role models. Susan Adcox writes about being a role model in her article, "10 Ways to be a Good Role Model for Grandkids," posted on The Spruce website. I kept her points and added comments from my experience.

How to Be a Good Role Model

- **Keep moving.** Don't become a couch potato. If you're already a couch potato, get up and get moving.

- **Develop a healthy relationship with food.** Eat moderately, not too little, and not too much. Overeating can be a sign of stress.

- **Accept your appearance; you're one of a kind.** Don't let TV and print ads determine your appearance.

- **Give to others.** Even if you have little to give, surely there is something to give, such as the gift of listening.

- **Put people above possessions.** You have obviously put a precious grandchild above yourself.

- **Be aware of the beauty that surrounds you.** Each day, stop for a minute and observe this beauty.

- **Have an optimistic attitude, even in tough times.** This may be a good time to read the notes in your Happiness Jar.

- **Monitor the tone of your voice.** This idea has been discussed previously, and is important.

- **Get interested in politics.** You can be informed and up-to-date without getting involved or strident.

- **"Forgive and forgive again."**

You don't need a teaching degree to be a life teacher; you already have many things to share. Put parent conferences on the calendar and plan to attend them. Help with homework as best you can. Learn about child development and how kids of different ages approach things. Connect with your grandchild's school and attend school functions. The best thing you can do for your grandkids is to encourage them to learn. Keep learning. Some of my friends do crossword puzzles to keep their minds active. I write articles and books.

These tips will help you stay active mentally, physically, and emotionally. Stand back, world. A dedicated, determined, and loving grandparent is on the job!

What Works

1. Find ways to participate at school.

2. Answer key questions before choosing a preschool.

3. Take steps to overcome school barriers.

4. Keep track of school expenses.

5. Help with homework, but don't provide all the answers.

6. Encourage your grandchild to join after-school activities.

7. Attend parent-teacher conferences if you feel comfortable doing so.

8. Think of yourself as a life teacher.

9. Try to be a good role model.

10. Share your education, talents, and skills with your grandchild.

CHAPTER 7

Stress and Its Impact

For people who are looking at your family from the outside, raising a grandchild looks like a straightforward job. If you take care of the basics, your grandchild will be happy. But millions of grandparents have learned that being a GRG or GAP is a complex, stressful role. The stress just keeps on coming. Karin Kisdin examines stress in her *Huffington Post* article, "Grandparents Raising Grandchildren: 'Twice the Stress of Average Parents.'" Some grandparents see their children's failure as their failure, Kisdin begins. "When they think of themselves as sub-par parents, they fret that they will shortchange their grandchildren in some way," she writes.

Fret is an interesting word choice here. The dictionary defines *fret* as visible and constant worry. Constant worry causes more stress. John and I were stressed because four family members had died within six months. Then, too, our lives had changed drastically. We went from a semi-retired lifestyle to raising teenagers, which can be a challenge under the best of circumstances. Raising the twins changed every aspect of our lives.

Although GRGs and GAPs have similar tasks, families can differ significantly. You may be raising one grandchild, and another grandfamily may be raising two or three. Caring for several grandchildren takes more effort than caring for one. The American Association for Marriage and Family Therapy, in a website article "Grandparents Raising Grandchildren," says some grandparents are still trying to help their grandchild's parents—no easy task. You may be in this situation.

I know parents who wanted to convince their child, the mother of their grandchild, to get treatment for addiction. The parents weren't successful. You may pay off your adult child's debts to protect the family name. You may put a new roof on your adult child's house because you want your grandchild to be snug, warm, and sheltered. "Grandparents may feel anger at their grandchildren's parents, guilt about their parenting, or embarrassment about their family situation," the article explains, an observation that is often true.

Pain of a Child in Pain

Raising a grandchild is hard, and your mixed feelings make it harder. One of the worst things you may see is a grandchild in emotional pain. Even if your grandchild didn't lose both parents, as the twins did, your emotional pain is substantial. Your grandchild may pick up on your pain. Can you withstand dual pain—a grandchild in pain and being in pain yourself? Time and again, I wished I could have felt the twins' pain for them. Life has its painful experiences, and they come to us all, no matter how old we are or how much pain we have already experienced. Because I've had a challenging life, I know the only way to get through pain is to accept it. The acceptance of pain shortens its duration— at least, that is my experience.

A grandchild in deep emotional pain may develop behavior problems. Before, your grandchild may have been calm, and now she or he argues constantly. Seeing your grandchild like this makes you suffer. Steven Stosny, PhD, examines suffering in his Psychology Today website article, "Pain and Suffering." Emotional pain is the body's life-saving alarm system, according to Stosny, and keeps us focused on distress. This focus makes us take steps to relieve stress.

You may be suffering now. This isn't a time for blame, resentment, or self-medication with with alcohol or other methods. Instead, it is a time to slow down and identify your feelings. Can you identify them? This isn't an easy question to answer because feelings can overlap. A trusted friend or relative may be able to name feelings for you—anger, resentment, despair, etc.

In "The Meaning of Emotional Pain," another Psychology Today website article, Stosny offers some coping steps. First, he thinks we need to ask ourselves "how" and not "why." How did my grandchild wind up living with me? Answering this question requires introspection and remembering. The "how" approach can keep you from magnifying emotional pain. You couldn't control the things that happened, and that's the truth. Avoid the blame-anger response—blaming everyone and getting angry about it—because it can lead to chronic resentment.

Although we can't control what happens in life, we can control the meaning of what happened. Stosny's approach: "I can recognize that I have the strength, resilience, and value to heal this hurt over time." You have the strength and resilience to help your grandchild. John and I didn't make a detailed plan to help the twins; we simply followed our instincts. These tips from my experience may help you, starting with listening.

First, you need to listen constantly and carefully. Your grandchild's conversation may give you hints about what is bothering her or him. The car is one of the best places for listening because the kids are contained. Listen for feeling words and signal words.

Be patient with your grandchild. Children's feelings can change quickly. One minute you may see tears and the next minute you may hear laughter. While you're practicing patience with your grandchild, please be patient with yourself. I wish I could say I did this all the time, but I didn't. John thinks I tend to be hard on myself, and he should know.

Find some outlets for your grandchild. These outlets may be family gatherings, sports, or art experiences. The next section of this chapter explains how art helps children heal. Art can be calming for children and revealing for adults.

Talk with your grandchild's guidance counselor. Tell the counselor about your grandchild's feelings. When I visited the twins' high school, I felt all of their teachers were familiar with our loss and cared about our family. This was reassuring.

Get professional counseling if you think your grandchild needs it. You don't have to sign up for long-term counseling; a few sessions may be helpful. Being able to talk with an understanding person to ventilate feelings helps your grandchild.

Watch for behavior problems. If your grandchild's behavior is out of control or is unusual, seek professional help. The Department of Social Services in your community, the school guidance counselor, or your religious community will be able to provide leads.

Learning to cope with pain is a life skill. An article on the Livestrong website, "List of Life Skills Children Should Have," says these skills include financial management, teamwork, etiquette, and managing emotions. Young as they are, toddlers and preschoolers can learn to manage their emotions. When I was teaching nursery school, I asked students not to use their hands for hitting, but to use their words instead. Every student responded well to this suggestion and was able to follow it.

Just like adults, some children manage emotions well and other times they "lose it." You can help by reading calming stories, providing art materials, exposing your grandchild to nature, and connecting her or him with your religious community. An older grandchild may wish to keep a journal. A young child may wish to draw pictures or write a story about their experiences. You may ask a very young grandchild to draw a picture and add the story as she or he tells it.

When I was teaching, I asked students to complete comics pages. I provided paper with dialogue "balloons" on them. The kids added drawings and dictated the dialogue to me.

This activity was so much fun that the kids asked for more comics pages.

Remember, your grandchild is watching you and gathering data constantly—information about your traits, values, coping skills, evaluation skills, problem-solving abilities, respect for others, and reliability. Bit by bit, these observations teach your grandchild how to cope. Years from now, your grandchild will remember your example. "You're funny when you're mad, Grandma," my granddaughter once observed. This was an interesting comment because I rarely get angry. In fact, anger is a glitch in my normal behavior.

Behavior Problems

While you're caring for your grandchild you need to watch for unhealthy coping mechanisms—conscious or unconscious behaviors that give a person a sense of control or comfort. Your grandchild may start twirling or pulling their hair, for example, which can be annoying to watch. Think about your grandchild's experiences. Has your grandchild been bullied? Is she or he short of friends? Your grandchild's behavior problems are a source of stress. Get help if it is too much to handle.

"Bad Habits/Annoying Behavior," an article posted on the University of Michigan Health System website, describes annoying behaviors. For some children, pulling hair is self-calming behavior.

If your grandchild is creating bare spots on the scalp, she or he may have a psychological problem that requires professional help.

Facial tics, such as blinking eyes, may be a problem for your grandchild. Temporary tics like this start in early childhood and the teen years, according to the University of Michigan, and last from one month to a year. Nose-twitching and grimacing are also facial tics, and they affect facial muscles.

Breath-holding is one of the scariest behavior problems for grandparents. Young children have been known to hold their breath until they pass out. These spells usually happen between the ages of eighteen and twenty-four months. The problem with breath-holding is that it can resemble a seizure. The University of Michigan article says you should take a child to the doctor if you've observed breath-holding behavior.

Traumatized youngsters, older children, and teens may develop oppositional defiant disorder (ODD). These children are angry, argue all the time, and are blatantly defiant. Ordinary days can become a battle when a grandchild has ODD. The American Academy of Child and Adolescent Psychiatry (AACAP) says all children can have this disorder from time to time. This behavior surfaces when kids are tired, hungry, stressed, or upset, according to the academy. Two-year-olds are famous for this behavior.

On your grandparenting journey, watch for symptoms of ODD: temper tantrums, excessive arguing, questioning rules, defiant behavior, trying to annoy others, anger and resentment, using mean and hateful words, spite, and revenge. The causes of ODD are still unknown, and the AACAP recommends a comprehensive evaluation if a child has some of these behaviors. Programs for parents and grandparents and medication management are solutions to consider. Here are some ways to help from the academy:

Build on positives. Praise your grandchild when she or he is flexible and cooperative. Again, be brief. "You have the neatest room in town!" is an example of a brief compliment.

Take a break. Tell your grandchild that you're going to take a short break to read a magazine or have a cup of tea. Ask your grandchild to take a break at the same time.

Pick your battles. The academy uses the example of time out. Ignore the arguing and tell your grandchild time out begins when she or he is in their room.

Set age-appropriate limits. All limits should have consequences. For example, a teenage grandchild may go to the concert if she or he does their laundry.

Retain interests and hobbies. You need to maintain your identity while you're raising your grandchild. Although you can't keep every interest or hobby, you can retain one or two.

Manage personal stress. "Me Time" and physical activity need to be part of every day. A fifteen-minute walk in the neighborhood can lift your spirits. Brief walks also connect you with nature.

Healing Power of Art

I minored in art when I was in college and have a graduate degree in art, so I'm an art booster. We always had crayons, drawing paper, water colors, water color markers, and sketching pencils in the house. As our daughters grew older, we did art activities together: creating shrink art (popular at the time), decorating melamine plates, making clothespin people, drawing, painting, creating salt-dough sculptures, and making suncatchers. When there aren't enough words, or words fail, art helps children to express their feelings.

I asked my nursery school students to draw angry pictures. While the kids were drawing they chatted about what made them angry, such as a sibling breaking a toy. Red and black were the dominant colors, and many drawings were toothy. One boy drew a picture of himself snarling. His oversized, fang-like teeth dominated the drawing, and were so threatening I expected them to jump off the paper and bite me. The kids enjoyed drawing angry pictures, and I was fascinated by their drawings.

Art therapist Marge Heegaard created a series of therapy books for children. The topics of her books include terrible events, divorce, self-control, illness, the death of a pet, and more.

What is art therapy? According to the American Art Therapy Association, it is a mental health profession that uses the creative process to "enhance the physical, mental, and emotional well-being of individuals of all ages." Art therapists work in hospitals, hospices, schools, and private practices. Art therapy books aren't the same as the adult coloring books that are so popular now. Adult coloring books divert and calm the mind with repetitive activity. Users add color to existing drawings.

In contrast, art therapy has no existing drawings, and people create their own. You don't have to be a certified art therapist to help your grandchild. Gather some art supplies, and store them in an accessible container, drawer, or closet. A plastic cleaning caddy with a handle is a good storage box. You can get one at a discount store for a few dollars. A shoe box also works. Your grandchild should be able to use art supplies at any time. Visiting an art museum is also a fun activity; many have free guided tours for children.

Exposing your grandchild to beauty may also be healing. Grandchildren often see beauty that adults miss. To a young child, a dandelion is beautiful and, when you examine its structure, you see your grandchild is right. Beauty surrounds us, yet we often take it for granted.

Priest and poet John O'Donohue examines beauty in depth in his book *The Invisible Embrace of Beauty*. Throughout the book, he spells beauty with a capital B. "When we lose sight of Beauty our struggle becomes tired and functional," he observes. "When we expect and engage the Beautiful, a new fluency is set within us and between us." O'Donohue believes our encounters with beauty restore hope and unexpected courage.

Take a walk with your grandchild and search for beauty. Count the beautiful things you see. You may also take photos with a smartphone. When you get home, you will feel refreshed, hopeful, and ready for another day.

One year on the first official day of spring in Rochester when it still felt like winter, I went outside and searched for beauty. A few piles of snow remained. Grass that had been covered by snow for months was starting to turn green. The tree in our front yard had tiny buds on it. Across the street, a red-winged blackbird was perched on a rooftop, calling to other birds. Two ribbon clouds were in the sky, one the palest pink, and the other a faded blue. A flock of geese flew overhead, honking as they made their way in V formation. Behind our townhome, sparrows and red-winged blackbirds were eating at our feeders. All of these were signs of spring and signs of hope.

Outside Interference

We heard many "you should" statements from people outside of the family while we were on our GRG journey. Statements are one thing; actions are another. One family whom we didn't even know crossed our family boundaries, and their interference lasted for months. Maybe they thought we were too old. Maybe they thought we were senile. Maybe they thought we were incapable of raising teenagers. Whatever the reason, their actions were inappropriate. John and I felt angry and hurt. I can't supply any more details about this situation for legal reasons.

Apparently these people thought they were helping us when they were actually harming us. They caused harm to our entire family. Outside interference can come from people who aren't raising their grandchildren. Well-meaning people see the family from the outside, not the inside, and the picture may not be clear. What they know or think they know can be skewed or false. Outside interference can be a wrecking ball that fractures the trust you have with your grandchild. What can you say to someone who jumped into your life uninvited?

Thanks for the idea. I'll give it some thought.

We have already taken care of the problem, but thank you.

Our grandchild is getting the care and support that she (he) needs.

I appreciate your concern, but this conversation is making me uncomfortable.

You are crossing our family boundaries. Please stop.

Your interference is hurting our family.

If you don't stop interfering, I will talk to a lawyer.

Notice that these statements get stronger and stronger. Sadly, you may get interference from your grandchild's parents. Millie Ferrer-Chancy and her colleagues examine this issue in their article "Grandparents Raising Grandchildren: Understanding Relationships," posted on the University of Florida website. You can diffuse the situation by not jumping to conclusions, saying unkind words, or placing blame, the authors note. Instead, you can be an active listener and try to see things from the other person's viewpoint. "Agree to disagree if you are unable to resolve conflict right away," the authors conclude.

Yet as often as you try and, as much as you hope, your efforts may be unsuccessful. The only thing you can do is let go. Letting go is a process, not an event, and happens gradually. Grandparents don't have to fix everything, according to Ferrer-Chancy and her colleagues. Remember, your child made their own choices, and experienced the consequences of those choices. For peace of mind, and legal protection, you may wish to write a Memorandum for Record. This is a dated narrative with brief descriptions. List the date first, followed by several sentences about what happened. Make your narrative brief and to the point.

Consult a lawyer if the outside interference doesn't stop. John and I asked our minister for help. She listened attentively and made a few suggestions. We also increased our grandparenting efforts. A month went by. The twins settled in more, became part of the family, and we referred to them as "our kids." Although the outside interference eventually stopped, we still feel the pain of that time.

Health Care and Stress

Extra medical and dental bills can be another source of stress. Your insurance may not cover your grandchild's health care bills. We were fortunate. The twins' father, a master electrician, had health coverage through his union. His plan covered the twins, and they carried their insurance cards with them. Thank goodness. One summer our grandson drove to Florida with friends to visit a buddy who had joined the military. While they were playing disc golf, his friend lost a disc, and our grandson went to look for it. Our grandson accidentally ran into a palm frond, and the jagged edge of the leaf scratched his cornea.

He called home for advice. John asked him to describe his symptoms, told him to wait an hour, and call back. The second call confirmed the scratched cornea. We were very worried because we knew a large scratch could become a harmful scar and impede our grandson's vision. John told him to go to the nearest hospital emergency room. He followed this advice and received excellent care, thanks in part to his insurance card. By the time our grandson returned home, his eye had almost healed.

"How many grandkids can call their grandpa and get medical advice?" I asked.

"No kidding," our grandson replied. The twins were glad to have a doctor in the house, and I was as well.

K.R. Tremblay and colleagues discuss health insurance in their Colorado State University website article "Grandparents: As Parents." Some grandkids are covered by the Civilian Health and Medical Program of the Uniformed Services (CHAMPUS), the article notes, but this insurance may not apply to the grandchild living in your home and under your care. CHAMPUS is similar to Medicare, and the government contracts private parties to administer this care.

A growing grandchild needs dental care. Our grandson had his wisdom teeth removed, and the procedure was covered by his father's insurance plan. The plan covered the twins as long as they were students. Many colleges and universities have student medical and dental plans. The University of Minnesota, for example, requires full-time students to have health insurance, and has some restrictions on how this insurance may be used. Students may also get private insurance or enroll in a group plan. Your local dental society should be able to provide some insurance advice. There may also be a free dental clinic in your town.

Stress of Raising Grandkids

Stress seems to come with the GRG territory. Your tasks never end, stamina wanes, and the bills keep coming. While you can't avoid stress, you can take steps to manage it. This needs to be a top priority. Lawrence Robinson, Melinda Smith, MS, and Robert Segal, MA, offer tips for controlling stress in their Help Guide website article "Stress Management: Simple Tips to Get Stress in Check and Regain Control of Your Life." You put your life at risk if you fail to manage stress, according to the authors. They say stress disturbs your emotional equilibrium and physical health. What's more, stress interferes with your ability to think clearly and enjoy life.

To manage stress you need to know its sources. Look for the real sources, and don't try to explain stress away by saying it's temporary. Stress will continue to build unless you identify your stressors. Indeed, your stress may get out of control. The authors of the article think keeping a journal may be helpful. Your entries should answer five questions. I kept the points of their questions, but changed the wording a bit. The list includes two additional questions from my caregiving experience.

1. What caused your stressful feelings?

2. How did you feel at the time?

3. How did you respond?

4. What steps did you take to feel better?

5. Is this a recurring cause of stress?

6. Has stress affected your blood pressure?

7. Are you taking blood pressure medication?

Robinson and his colleagues suggest a four-step approach to dealing with stress: avoid, alter, adapt, and accept. Avoidance was easy for me. I didn't watch many television newscasts, avoided grumpy people, and read upbeat articles and books. John is fascinated by World War II and I asked him not to watch war programs before bedtime. Acceptance was hard for us. I could hardly believe four family members had died, and it was difficult to accept these losses. "Don't try to control the uncontrollable," Robinson and his colleagues advise. It's good advice for all GRGs and GAPs.

Relaxation techniques help to reduce stress, and one technique is diaphragm breathing. This works for me and may work for you. Jeanette Moniger offers more de-stressing ideas in her WebMD article "10 Relaxation Techniques that Zap Stress Fast." Her ideas include meditation, five-minute deep-breathing breaks, living mindfully, being aware of your body, warm wraps, physical activity, and gratefulness. You may want to keep a gratitude journal. Seeing what you're grateful for in writing imprints these things in your mind.

Bring up the topic of stress in a GRG support group. How are other grandparents coping with it? What are their best tips? Sharing ideas with people who understand your life can be a stress-reduction starting point. Besides, it feels good to let your feelings out.

Accepting kindness may also reduce stress. I think kindness is a gift, and we received many gifts of kindness while we were raising the twins. One family invited our granddaughter over for dinner before gymnastics practice. Grief was new and raw for our granddaughter the first time she went to her friend's home. When she pulled up in front of the house, family members were standing outside to welcome her.

"Everyone in the family—even their grandma—was standing on the lawn," our granddaughter recalled. "It was so sweet!"

Our extended family provided emotional support for us. We knew the first Thanksgiving without Helen would be difficult because she was born on Thanksgiving. To ease our pain, family members decided to have Thanksgiving dinner at our niece's home. At the time, she and her husband were living on a hobby farm. The children played with the goats, chickens, and dogs. Celebrating Thanksgiving in a new place lowered our stress, although tears were always close. We received so many thoughtful gifts of kindness that John and I could have sobbed for days.

You may have received gifts of kindness. These gifts comforted you and, even better, you may pass them on someday. Thank people for their gifts of kindness. I write thank-you notes (my mother trained me well), send thank-you emails, or send people one of my books. Kindness can change an entire day.

Don't be afraid to ask for help. You may contact your religious community and ask for some meals to be delivered, or help with housekeeping tasks.

The following tips will help to reduce the stress of grandparenting, and keep you on an even, forward path.

What Works

1. Use your strength and resilience to help your grandchild.

2. Take steps to cope with the pain of a child in stress.

3. Watch for your grandchild's coping mechanisms.

4. Keep art materials on hand.

5. Take walks with your grandchild and look for beauty.

6. Get professional help for Oppositional Defiant Disorder.

7. Counter outside interference that harms the family.

8. Get health care and dental insurance for your grandchild.

9. Take steps to reduce and control stress.

10. Use the four-A plan to combat stress: avoid, alter, adapt, accept.

11. Be willing to accept kindness from relatives and friends.

CHAPTER 8

Boosting Children's Goals and Dreams

A goal is something you want to get to, get done, or do better. As children grow, their dreams can shift and change. A four-year-old granddaughter may have wanted to be a ballerina; as she grew older, she discovered she didn't have the talent or stamina to pursue this career. A grandson may have dreamed of becoming a professional tennis player. After playing on the school team, he realized he was good at tennis but not good enough for a professional team. Disappointments don't stop grandchildren from setting goals, and their old dreams are replaced by new ones. Teenagers can have lofty goals, such as saving the world from pollution. Breaking this goal down into parts—collecting plastic bottles, having a newspaper drive, picking up trash from highways—makes it more attainable. Our goal for the twins was to provide a loving, stable home. The twins set their own goals. I think their top goal was to get good grades. John and I wanted them to excel, but we didn't push them; the twins pushed themselves. I had never seen kids work so hard.

Make sure your grandchild's goals are their goals, not yours. Your grandchild may want to be an engineer, pilot, or poet. The goal needs to come from your grandchild, and she or he needs to own it. Pushing a grandchild toward a different goal, one they don't care about or want, could create problems in the future.

Recently I heard a story about a little girl who wanted to be an artist. Her parents didn't want her to do that, so the girl went into a completely different field. When she reached middle age, however, she decided to make her dream come true, took some lessons, and is an accomplished artist today.

Goal-Setting Steps

The start of a new school year is an ideal time for goal setting. Amelia Morin examines the process in her article, "Setting Back to School Goals," posted on The Spruce website. She thinks setting goals is more than taking steps to get what you want. Goal setting is a process that helps children gain independence and control. Although your grandchild is dependent on you now, you want to foster their independence. You want your grandchild to have a good life. Morin says parents (and grandparents) can help children set goals by listening, helping with vocabulary, and helping to refine unrealistic goals. Rather than saying a goal is unrealistic, you and your grandchild may want to divide it into smaller steps. Let's say your grandchild wants to be a figure skater. The first goal is to move on skates without falling. The second goal is to pick up speed and glide. The third goal is to learn to spin, and so on. After you've done this together, determine if the smaller goals will work for your grandchild.

Setting goals is similar to going on a trip. Your grandchild needs to know the destination, and make preparations. You may want a toddler grandchild to be potty trained before a trip. Although a child this age doesn't understand goal setting, you can work on it together. While preteens and teens are able to understand goal-setting steps, they may still need adult help. "How to Teach Kids Perseverance and Goal-Setting," an article by Marie Faust Evitt, offers some tips for parents and grandparents. She cautions adults about getting too excited.

"You probably won't be able to get your child to start aiming for straight As right away," she writes. She advises parents (and grandparents) to start with something a child can do, such as saving money. Fun goals are easier to work for and can be achieved in a shorter time, according to Evitt. It's a good idea to talk with your grandchild about what it will take to reach their goal. You and your grandchild may make a plan together.

Visuals will help your grandchild remember the plan. For example, a young child will enjoy a magazine picture of a child riding a two-wheel bike. An older grandchild may like arrows drawn from one goal-setting step to another. Another option is to take your grandchild to a sports store and pick out a piece of equipment to attain his or her goal. When a child falls short of a goal, Evitt says you should review it, ask for ideas, focus on benefits, talk out frustrations, and praise efforts.

Her article ends with five goal-setting steps. The first is to put the goal in writing. For a kindergartener, first or second grader, please use manuscript printing, not cursive writing. The second step is to make the goal specific. One short sentence about the goal will make it easy for your grandchild to remember. Next, consider the pros and cons of the goal. You may need several conversations in order to do this. Then it's time to define the steps, using Evitt's "W" approach: Who can help? What does my grandchild need to do? When will my grandchild work on the goal? Finally, monitor your grandchild's progress.

Goal setting is a sign of hope, a belief that life will get better, and you need to nurture this belief. Daniel Goleman writes about the link between goals and hope in his book *Emotional Intelligence: Why It Can Matter More Than I.Q.* To hope means you won't give in to overwhelming anxiety, self-defeating thoughts, depression, or the setbacks of life, according to Goleman. He believes that hopeful people have less depression. Goal setting is hard if your grandchild's life has been disrupted, but this doesn't mean goal setting is impossible.

The process begins with objectives. A stressed grandchild may not be able to focus on objectives, and you may have to help. Instead of thinking of several objectives, think of one. Help your grandchild answer these questions: What is my goal? Why is it important? Is my goal reasonable? What steps do I need to take to achieve my goal? Some people set deadlines for their goals, but this may be too much for your grandchild.

I was constantly amazed at how hard the twins studied. As soon as they came home from school, they went to their rooms and started their homework. Sometimes my grandson wouldn't get the grade he anticipated on a test. He was matter-of-fact about this. "I'm not worried," he said. "I'll work on it." This has been his approach all through high school, college, and graduate school.

I think reaching goals is easier with a team approach. Your grandchild will try harder knowing you are rooting for her or him and ready and willing to help. Do all you can to help your grandchild accomplish her or his goals. This may involve carpooling, buying supplies, or helping with group projects. The twins' high school fostered the group approach. Students would meet together, do independent research, and write a group report together.

My granddaughter's group was small but mighty. "Can my group spend the night, Grandma?" she asked. "We have to finish our project." I agreed to the sleepover, and a few hours later, six giggling girls walked in the door. John and I had to move the Ping-Pong table aside to make room for all the sleeping bags. The girls worked well into the night. This was group effort in action and, at the same time, fun for the girls.

Your grandchild may benefit from goal-setting worksheets, and many are available on the Internet. Use the search words *setting goals worksheets* and see what appears. I found worksheets on basic goals, clarifying goals, mindset, a goal survey, habits, and action. One worksheet linked goals with change, a logical approach. Another worksheet helped a child rate their goals. Worksheets like these are helpful for all kids, but especially visual learners. Have a small celebration when your grandchild reaches a goal.

Free Time and Fun

Young children learn by playing. Before your grandchild came to live with you, their play may have been limited. Put original play—unstructured play created by her or him—on the daily schedule. You may join your grandchild's play, but do it at their level. Our backyard was fairly steep. One fall when the twins were in kindergarten or first grade, I showed them how to roll down the grassy bank. I rolled down first, and the twins followed me. Our house was at the bottom of a hill and if neighbors looked out their windows, they would see me rolling. I pictured them watching me, shaking their heads, and saying, "The poor dear. Harriet has finally lost it."

I hadn't lost it and loved rolling down the hillside with the twins. Fall had come. We smelled it in the air, and heard it in the papery leaves as we rolled over them. While we rolled, more leaves fell from the two-hundred-year-old oak trees in our yard. When we finished rolling, I gave the twins rakes, and they raked leaves into piles. This memory, an example of original play with adult participation, is still clear in my mind. All these years later, I feel the joy of that day.

John contributed to play by building a seesaw for the twins.

Each Sunday, when Helen and the twins came for dinner, they checked the progress of his work. Several weeks passed, and the twins waited impatiently for their seesaw. "Grandpa is building a park," our grandson announced in a low, serious voice. The twins enjoyed the seesaw once it was finished and took turns using the swing that hung from the deck. We also took the twins to our neighborhood park and went for walks.

Today, many children and grandchildren aren't getting the physical activity they need. Worse, original play is under attack, according to the article "Child's Play: Importance of Play Time for Children Neglected, Advocates Say" on the Town Talk website. Since the 1970s children have lost an average of nine hours of free play per week. Do the math. Nine hours a week, multiplied by fifty-two weeks in a year, adds up to 468 hours a year. These hours of joyful learning are lost forever. This fact makes me think of a conversation I had with my sister-in-law.

Her house was on a hillside that overlooked a flat parcel of land in the valley below. Family members became concerned when a developer bought the parcel, laid out blocks, paved the streets, and started to build dozens of houses. "We thought the sound of the neighbors below would be disruptive," my sister-in-law commented. "But we never heard a sound, and we never saw a child. All the parents were working." To me, this was a sad commentary on modern life. Young children need to be outdoors, moving around, in touch with nature, and enjoying original play.

I understand why kids aren't outside. The world is a more dangerous place today, and parents can't be blamed for worrying about their children's safety. Still, I make a case for original play. It helps children solve problems, make decisions, learn new words, build relationships, and handle disappointments. I think original play helps children create their identities. "The Importance of Human Play in Human Development," an article on the Playing by Heart website, lists some of the many benefits of play. This kind of play reduces fear, anxiety, stress, and irritability, the article explains, and is a healing time for children. Social benefits include sharing, compassion, and empathy. The physical benefits include improved range of motion, balance, and fine motor skills. Brain function becomes more efficient as well.

Although you may join in your grandchild's play, let your grandchild guide the play and dialogue. Pay attention to what your grandchild is saying. Instead of hurrying things along, let the play evolve and develop at its own place. If you need to intervene, be gentle and speak in a calm voice. You may also sit nearby and watch the play. Your grandchild will figure out what's fun for her or him.

Photography was, and continues to be, our granddaughter's passion. We did everything we could to support this interest. John gave her some of his old camera lenses. We delivered submission forms and photos to fair officials. Our granddaughter won two prizes at the Minnesota State Fair and the county fair. One of her photos, a close-up of half a cow's face, won a blue ribbon at the state fair. I would have photographed the entire cow's face, but the judges thought half a face was more captivating. It's a great shot.

You may wish to arrange for private lessons if you think your grandchild is talented. A retired teacher may be willing to give free lessons. Scouting programs may also provide training. The local art museum may have a summer art camp for children. Our granddaughter participated in a high school mentoring program and received free lessons from a local photographer. Our grandson wanted to learn how to play his late father's guitar, a vintage instrument that turned out to be valuable. We gave him guitar lessons for Christmas. Although he didn't take lessons for a long time, he had the satisfaction of using the guitar and making music.

How to Give Constructive Criticism

One of the hardest things for adults to learn is how to guide without wounding a child. One critical comment can be a lasting blow for a grandchild. "You're off to a good start" is one positive lead-in sentence. What can you say after that? The Toolbox Talk website offers tips in the article "Constructive Criticism: Giving It . . . and Receiving It!" Constructive criticism is essential for quality performance, the article notes, and gains from this criticism can be substantial. "Firmness might be necessary," the article explains. These steps will help you provide constructive criticism.

- **Acknowledge the positive.** State what is right and good about the situation. Comment on what your grandchild has done so far.

- **Provide quality feedback.** Be clear, and remind your grandchild of the goal, and the expected outcome. Encourage your grandchild, but don't exaggerate.

- **Remain calm.** While it's normal to be anxious about criticizing your grandchild, you can speak in a calm voice. You may have to repeat your comment.

I think you need to give yourself and your grandchild a break. Working toward a goal is sequential. It's unrealistic to expect instantaneous results. Setbacks are part of goal setting too and grandkids need to learn this.

Fostering a grandchild's goals and dreams requires extra effort. You may think you're doing well only to find out you're not. Everyone in the family has up and down feelings. Ignoring the small stuff will help you survive.

Jim Fay and Foster W. Cline, MD, offer some tips for coping with up and down emotions in their book *Grandparenting with Love & Logic*. These tips are written with divorce in mind, but may be applied to grandparents raising grandkids. One tip is to avoid criticizing our grandchild's parents, something already discussed in this book. Another is to praise your grandchild. The twins did many things for us, such as sweeping the garage and taking out the trash. We appreciated their efforts.

Messes can be cleaned up. Dirty clothes can wait until another day. The place won't collapse if you don't dust the furniture. Errands can be postponed. Sometimes you have to call time out, sit down, and take a well-deserved rest. You can resume working on goals tomorrow.

Making Progress

Our grandfamily had melded together and we were making progress. You will have days when you wonder if you're making any progress. Does your grandchild seem happy? Are you happy with their progress? At first, the twins didn't talk very much. As the months passed they became more verbal. Several years after they moved in with us they were bubbly and excited about school. Our behavior probably matched theirs. Gauging the emotional atmosphere in the house will give you an indication of progress.

Sleeping well is one indication. Your grandchild may have had nightmares when she or he came to live with you. Nightmares are upsetting for young children. If your grandchild awakens crying from a dream, comfort them, give lots of hugs, and leave a light on. You may also find other "huggies" for your grandchild, such as a well-loved teddy bear or blanket. Check under the bed for monsters, and assure your grandchild that none are hiding there. The absence of nightmares and the return of restful sleep are signs of progress.

Reading body language—the unconscious response to what is being said or taking place—is another way to tell if you're making progress. Susan Krauss Whitbourne, PhD, lists key aspects of body language in her Psychology Today website article, "The Ultimate Guide to Body Language." The head, torso, legs, and feet are things to watch. A straight back is a sign of confidence and control, according to Whitbourne, whereas a sagging back signals that the person doesn't feel good about themselves. Fidgeting hands can be an indication of boredom or anger. Foot tapping or unconscious leg shaking are signs of irritation or anxiety.

The body's actions reflect what is going on in the mind. A few of the cited behaviors are nothing to worry about. If your grandchild has none of them, you're doing a great job.

Conversation can be an indication of progress. Listen to your grandchild's word choices. Negative words can be a signal of anxiety and sadness. Examples of negative words are *can't, won't, angry, boring, mean, hurt, nasty, nobody, ugly, upset,* and *stinky.* Listen for positive words too: *love, like, understand, happy, cool, fun, smart, joyous, creative,* and *safe.* A grandchild that uses more positive words than negative ones is making progress.

Several years ago I attended the regional conference of The Compassionate Friends, an international organization for parents and families that have suffered the loss of a child. I participated in a panel discussion, autographed books in the conference bookstore, and talked with people about my forthcoming book about happiness. "How do you know you're happy?" a woman asked. Talk about a pithy question! Details raced through my mind. Since giving her a complete answer would have taken an hour, I said my happy grandchildren made me happy. The woman was mystified.

I mentioned this conversation to Dr. Gloria Horsley, one of the founders of The Compassionate Friends. "I wasn't sure how to respond," I admitted.

"Think about where you were before," she suggested, "and think about where you are now." No doubt about it, the contrast was startling. Comparing the past to the present gives you an idea of your grandchild's progress. Your grandchild may be calmer now, and joking with you. An irresponsible grandchild may be more responsible. Your previously passive grandchild may be interested in everything. When you look at photos, you may see your grandchild is taller, looks happier, and looks healthier.

All of these things are rewards for being a GRG or GAP. With all that has happened, however, you may wonder if you are still you.

Who Am I Now?

The talents, education, and experience you had before you started raising your grandchild are still part of you. You haven't lost your identity; you have improved it. Better yet, you are enjoying life.

Katrina Kenison makes some important points in her book *The Gift of an Ordinary Day*. She describes the fast pace of her life. "Lately, I've noticed that when someone asks me how I'm doing, I reply by telling them how busy I've been," she writes. This sentence startled me because I've done the same thing. A balanced life has a rhythm, according to Kenison, and "a thoughtful life is not rushed."

Before I read her book I came to the same conclusion and consciously slowed my thoughts. This doesn't mean I was generally slow. I continued to write, only more thoughtfully. I continued to do my daily tasks, only more thoughtfully. I continued to volunteer, only more thoughtfully. Slowing my thoughts made me more aware of the strengths I brought to grandparenting.

There is no final answer to the question "Who am I now?" Like all grandparents and caregivers, I am continually evolving, and a work in progress. Being John's primary caregiver has changed me and continues to change me. The fact that John is alive is a miracle, and we celebrate this miracle daily. I've always been a person who cries easily, but now I'm also a person who celebrates easily.

Becoming GRGs was an easy decision for John and me. It came from love, and our love for the twins has buoyed us through hard times and kept us going. We are a grandfamily, and all of us are grateful. Many grandparents live far away from their grandchildren and don't get to see them often. We were glad the twins lived in Rochester. Becoming a GRG gave us the chance to know them and make something good from tragedy. Judy Tatelbaum thinks love is a source of courage, and makes this point in her book, *The Courage to Grieve.* "Having the courage to grieve is having the courage to live, to love, to risk," Tatelbaum writes. Our grandchildren gave us the courage to trust life again and enjoy each day.

Love can lead us and take us where we need to go. In the years to come, your grandchild may not remember everything about living with you but will remember your love. It really is the tie that binds. I think GRGs and GAPs need to celebrate their small and large successes. While we're at it, we may as well celebrate life. So get out the balloons, bring on the goodies, and cue the laughter. Celebration time has come.

Time to Celebrate!

"What happened to the twins?" I'm often asked this question and eager to answer it. They graduated from high school with honors. We had a graduation party for them. In Rochester, some high school graduation parties are elaborate. John and I opted for a simple ice cream social. All of the neighbors knew we were raising the twins. I printed out notices announcing their graduations and alerting them to extra traffic on the cul-de-sac. Our granddaughter's Girl Scout troop loaned us a large tent, and we positioned it next to the driveway. We were glad to have the tent when the sky turned dark and a few raindrops fell.

John and I guided the twins through the college search and tried not to interfere. Our grandson preferred large schools, whereas our granddaughter preferred small ones. After visiting several schools, our grandson was accepted at the University of Minnesota College of Neuroscience. Our granddaughter was accepted at Coe College in Cedar Rapids, Iowa, a small school that looks like a movie set.

Both of the twins graduated from college with high honors and Phi Beta Kappa. John wasn't able to attend their graduations, so I watched the ceremonies for both of us, noting as many details as I could and listening as attentively as I could. I went to our granddaughter's graduation first. The Coe College outdoor ceremony was impressive. Our granddaughter looked happy and pleased with her achievements.

The next weekend I attended our grandson's graduation at the University of Minnesota. The ceremony was held indoors. Family members had good seats and the ceremony opened with music by a brass trio. The instant I heard the first notes of the processional I began to cry. I turned around, saw our grandson in his robe and honors tassels, and cried harder. "We did it!" I exclaimed to the members of my family. "All of us did it!" It had taken the efforts of our entire family to get the twins across the finish line. Their efforts and determination counted, too, and it was a time of celebration.

To this day, I wish John had been able to attend the twins' college graduations.

When John heard the odds for surviving his third surgery, he was "willing to roll the dice," as he put it. One year after his aorta dissected, John, in his electric wheelchair, looking distinguished in a tweed jacket with a flower in the lapel and a wearing a gray patterned tie, escorted our granddaughter down the aisle on her wedding day. When I turned and saw our smiling grand-daughter holding onto John's arm as if he were walking, tears filled my eyes. People who knew our story were crying too. It was an emotional day for many of us.

Because John rolled the dice, he knows our granddaughter is an independent photographer and a foster mother for three children. Because John rolled the dice, he knows our grandson is a student at the Mayo Clinic School of Medicine in Rochester. He will be the third physician in our immediate family. Because John rolled the dice, he knows I wrote a series of books for family caregivers and served as medical consultant for the first one in the series, *The Family Caregiver's Guide.*

"I was willing to take a chance because I wanted more time with you," John has said many times. In August of 2017 we celebrated our sixtieth wedding anniversary, and treasure our days together. Our grandson often stops by to help us with computer glitches and comes for dinner with his girlfriend. Our granddaughter and her husband visit us when they have time. To my surprise and delight, the twins tell stories about living with us, and even quote us. "He talks about you a lot," my grandson's girlfriend shared. Our family connections are still strong, and I think they always will be.

Raising my grandchildren changed me, and being a GRG or GAP will change you. The benefits of your role may not be apparent now, but I can assure you of their existence. Give yourself credit for all you've done, and all you will do. Several years have passed since I was an active GRG, and I'm still learning about the benefits of this role. John and I know we made a difference in our grandchildren's lives. We are grateful for the opportunity to get to know the twins. Raising our grandkids made us stronger people. Some days we think we can hear the sound of their laughter. We fervently hope that we were good role models, and continue to be good role models for our precious twins.

Before I became a GRG I thought I was a strong person. I'm far stronger now. This strength has become part of my life, part of my thinking, and part of my problem-solving. The other day, as I was checking out of the grocery store, the sales associate asked if I had any coupons.

"No, I'm not that smart," I answered.

"I'm street smart!" the young man exclaimed.

"Well, I'm grandma smart," I replied, "and a force to be reckoned with."

"Wow!" he said with surprise.

Grandparents are a force to be reckoned with and our power is growing. Although there are millions of GRGs and GAPs across the nation and around the world, we need to be better connected. Reach out to other grandparents who are raising grandkids. Take advantage of grandparenting resources. Visit and learn from Internet communities and blogs. Our grandchildren come to us with a special gift and it is hope. In time, we have hope for our grandchildren, hope for ourselves, and hope for the future. Life is wonderful!

What Works

1. Focus on the positives of raising a grandchild.

2. Help your grandchild set goals.

3. Follow the goal-setting steps.

4. Learn how to give constructive criticism.

5. Enjoy free time and fun with your grandchild.

6. Watch for signs of progress in your grandchild.

7. Foster your grandchild's talents and interests.

8. Understand who you are now.

9. Take advantage of GRG and GAP resources.

10. Celebrate small and large successes.

11. Celebrate life.

Conclusion

Years have passed since the twins lived with us. Those years have taught me the most important life lesson: *love surmounts troubles and lasts forever.* John and I learned more from the twins than they learned from us. We didn't think the twins would understand how we helped them until they were in their forties, but we were wrong. So wrong. By the time they graduated from college the twins knew how we helped them. Today, they are helping us in more ways than we can count, and we are grateful. Here are some of the things we learned:

Grandkids make us laugh.

Grandkids are curious.

Grandkids enjoy learning and we can learn with them.

Grandkids want to explore.

Grandkids value friends.

Grandkids need kindness.

Grandkids practice kindness.

Grandkids enjoy giving to others.

Grandkids accept grandparents' mistakes.

Grandkids have serious goals.

Grandparents need to let go when the time comes.

You may be wondering if your grandchild or grandchildren will understand what you have done when they're older. Don't underestimate your grandchildren, for they can surprise you. Love is the greatest gift we have for our grandchildren, and similarly, receiving their love is the greatest gift for us. When they look back at this time, our grandkids will remember the loving things we did and the laughter we shared. You and your grandchild or grandchildren are making history together. This chapter of family history can influence future generations.

GRGs and GAPs like you and me are doing more than caring for grandchildren. We are changing the structure of families. Over time, these changes impact communities, states, and even nations. At this time in history, I think grandparents are needed more than ever. We are a stabilizing force in children's lives. We are a stabilizing force in the world. Think of what you have done and all you continue to do. These are things to remember, and I hope you're recording your family history in a diary, journal, photo montage, videos, or a memory book. You are a unique person and have things to say.

I think I kept my promise to write a book that contains support, guidance, and tested tips. Please read the appendixes and bibliography for more resources. For additional information, visit www.harriethodgson.com or send an email to harriethodgson@ charter.net. I will reply to your email as quickly as possible. You may wish to start a support group for grandparents raising grandchildren, give talks about your experiences, or write your own book. While raising your grandkids can be a challenge, it can also be one of the greatest joys of your life. Savor each day!

Appendix A

Some Helpful Websites

- **Administration on Aging,**
  www.aoa.gov/prof/notes/Docs/Grandparents_Raising_
  Grandchildren.pdf

- **American Association of Retired Persons (AARP),
  Grandparent Information Center,**
  www.aarp.org/families/grandparents

- **American Academy of Child and Adolescent Psychiatry,**
  www.aacap.org

- **American Bar Association Center for Children and Law,**
  www.abanet.org/child/home.html

- **American Grandparents Association,**
  https://grandparents.com/american-grandparents-
  association

- **American Psychological Association,**
  www.apa.org

- **Christian Legal Society,**
  www.clsnet.org

- **Grandparent Caregivers: A National Guide,**
  http://www.igc.org/justice/cjc/lspc/manual.cover.html

- **Grandparenting Foundation,**
  www.grandparenting.org

- **Grandparents as Parents,**
  http://home1.gte.net/res02two7

- **Grandparents Resource Center,**
  http://grc4usa.org

- **Grandparents Who Care,**
  www.grandparentswhocare.com

- **Intergenerational Connections,**
  http://www.nnfr.org/igen

- **National Center on Grandparents Raising Grandchildren,**
  www.chhs.gsu.edu/nationalcenter

- **National Legal Aid & Defender Association,**
  www.nlada.org

- **Social Security Benefits for Grandchildren,**
  www.ssa/gov/kids/parents5.htm

- **The American Self-Help Clearinghouse,**
  www.selfhelp-groups.org

- **The Compassionate Friends,**
  www.tcf.org

- **The Foundation for Grandparenting,**
  www.grandparenting.org

- **The Grandparents Rights Organization,**
  www.grandparentsrights.org

- **USA Government blog,**
  www.usa/gov/Topics/Grandparents.shtml

- **US Government Housing Assistance,**
  www.housingassistanceonline.com

Appendix B

A GRG's Bill of Rights by Harriet Hodgson

Grandparents who are raising their grandchildren have many rights. You may as well take advantage of them, and that's why I made this list. You have the right to

- Enjoy your grandchild each day.
- Feed your grandchild nutritious, balanced, colorful meals, and normal serving sizes.
- Give your grandchild a sandwich if she or he rejects dinner.
- Make play part of each day.
- Help with homework but don't provide answers.
- Teach your grandchild basic manners.
- Ask your grandchild to help around the house.
- Laugh at your own jokes even if they're sappy.
- Expect teens to provide who, what, when, where, why, and how details.
- Set reasonable bedtimes and curfews.
- Use the word no when necessary.
- Teach your grandchild how to budget and save money.
- Get your grandchild to clean up her or his bedroom and ignore the "moanie groanies."

- Require a driving grandchild to fill the gas tank when the gauge reads one-quarter full.

- Ask grandkids to turn the car radio back to your favorite station.

- Stop loud music and phone calls after 9:00 p.m.

- Repeat stories even if your grandchild rolls her or his eyes.

- Say, "I love you" every day.

Appendix C

10 Tips for Grandparents Raising Grandchildren

- Create a daily routine and stick with it as best you can.
- Eat healthy, nutritious, colorful meals. (Coffee and chips aren't a meal.)
- Put daily physical activity—walking, stretching, yoga—on your calendar.
- Turn off the television one hour before bedtime.
- Establish a bedtime routine and try to get seven hours of sleep a night.
- Join a GRG or GAP support group and/or online community.
- Stay in touch with friends.
- Have at least one meaningful conversation a day.
- Make "Me Time" a part of each day. You deserve it!
- Keep a Happiness Jar. Read the notes at year's end.

Appendix D

Words to Know

accumulated loss – stored, buried loss that flares without warning

active listening – intensive listening without interrupting

adoption – termination of parental rights; grants all rights and obligations for the care of a child to other people who aren't relatives; may pertain to grandparents

anniversary reaction – feelings of loss and grief sparked by a date, event, or experience

anticipatory grief – feeling of loss before a death or dreaded event occurs

art therapy – using art and the creative process to treat psychiatric and psychological problems

body language – unconscious body and head signals that reveal inner thoughts

caregiver – person who cares for another's needs, health, and well-being

conservator – legal designation given to an adult who grants her or him to manage a minor's finances; requires extensive reporting to the court

constructive criticism – providing feedback that will help the listener(s) with present and future tasks

creative outlets – experiences that reveal the person's inner thoughts and feelings such as writing, art, music, crafts, etc.

culture – one's beliefs, values, and customs

depersonalization – watching life from the outside without being personally involved

depression – feelings of despondency and pessimism about the future; a brain illness

denial – conscious or unconscious refusal to accept facts

diary – a daily written record of experiences and thoughts

ethnicity – refers to race

family caregiver – family member who cares for another family member short-term or long-term

goal – something you want to get to, get done, or do better

grandfamily – merging of grandparents and grandchildren into a family unit

granny nanny – grandmother who cares for a grandchild or grandchildren part-time

grief – a natural response to the death of a family member, loved one, friend, or pet; varies with the individual

grief reconciliation – acceptance of loss and returning to life

GAP – grandparent as parent

GRG – grandparent raising grandchildren

guardian – legal designation given to an adult granting her or him the responsibility for a minor's life

journal – a regularly written record of activities, thoughts, and ideas

kinship care – grandparent or other relative caring for a child

legal custody – custody granted to grandparents or other relatives if parents are unfit

letting go – a process of developing emotional detachment from a deceased loved one, living person, or circumstance

linking object – an object that links an individual with a deceased or absent person, such as a watch

loss history graph – linear representation of losses with dates of these losses

magical thinking – young child's tendency to mix reality with fantasy

Memo for Record – written record containing dates, events, and concerns; may be used in a court of law

multiple losses – many or successive deaths; requires longer recovery time than a single loss

peer group – influential group of people usually the same age

Power of Attorney – legal document that allows an adult to make decisions for another adult's welfare; does not include transfer of legal custody

preexisting condition – includes physical abuse, emotional abuse, neglect, exposure to drugs and alcohol, and loss of a parent due to death or imprisonment

oppositional defiant disorder (ODD) – angry, defiant, argumentative behavior in excess of what is normal

original play – non-structured play for children; adult may participate at the child's level of development

post traumatic stress disorder (PSTD) – a pattern of symptoms following a traumatic event; symptoms include anxiety, tension, nightmares, and depression

role reversal – mentally or actually adopting another person's role

self-care – steps taken by an individual to feel better

situational depression – temporary depression caused by a specific event or events

stressor – any upsetting change that has physical or emotional outcomes

projection – attributing one's own traits, attitudes, and faults to others

traumatic death – sudden and unanticipated loss; frequently violent, random, and preventable

values – standards accepted by an individual or society; desirable achievements

Bibliography

Note: Every effort has been made to ensure these links are current and viable. Over time, however, some links may have changed.

Adcox, Susan, "Asian Grandparents Have Influence, Status," posted on the About.com website, http://grandparents.aboout/com/od/grandparentingtoday/a/Asian grandparents.htm

Adcox, Susan, "Grandparents as Parents: GRGs/GAPs Have Major Issues to Resolve," posted on the About.com website, http://grandparents.about.com/od/grandparentingissues/tp/Raising/Grand.htm

Adcox, Susan, "10 Ways to be a Good Role Model for Grandkids," posted on The Spruce website, https://www.thespruce.com/good-role-model-for-grandkids-1696024

Adcox, Susan, "When Grandparenting Isn't Fun," posted on the About.com website, http://grandparents.about.com/od/grandparentingissues/a/GrandparentIssues.htm

Al-Azami, Dr. Salman and Byllenspetz, Ian, "Grandparents and Grandchildren Learning Together," www.grandparentsplus.org.uk/wp-content/uploads/2011/03/Schools

Allan, David M., M.D., "A Matter of Personality: From Borderline to Narcissism," posted on the "Psychology Today" website, http://

www.psychologytoday.com/blog/matter-personality/201106/
grandparents-raising-gr

American Academy of Child & Adolescent Psychiatry, "Grandparents Raising Grandchildren," posted on the AACAP website,
http://www.aacp.org/cs/root/facts

American Academy of Child & Adolescent Psychiatry, "Oppositional Defiant Disorder," posted on the AACP website, http://
www.aacp.org/AACP/Families_and_YouthFacts_for   Families
/FFF-Guide/Children-With-Oppositional-Defiant-Disorcer
-072.aspx

American Art Therapy Association, "The Association's Mission,"
posted on the American Art Therapy website, http://arttherapy.
org/aata-aboutus.html

American Association for Marriage and Family Therapy,
"Grandparents Raising Grandchildren," posted on the AAMFT
website, http://www.aamft.org.imis15/content/

Bales, Diane, "Grandparents Raising Grandchildren: Helping
Grandchildren Stay in Contact with Parents," University of
Georgia website, www.fcs.uga.edu/pubs/PDF/CHFD-E-59-2.
pdf,

Barauski, Sue, et al., "Improving Immigrant and Refugee
Families in Their Children's Schools: Barriers, Challenges, and
Successful Strategies," www.brycs.org/documents/upload/
InvolvingFamilies.pdf

Baxtor, Susan, "Grandparents As Teachers," posted on A Place of
Our Own website, www.aplaceofour own/org/question_detail.
php?id=365

Berman, Diane, PsyD, PCPC, "Supporting Your Teenager Through Grief and Loss," http://www.examiner.comspecial-needs-parent-in-washington-dc/supporting-your-teenager

Bolton, Robert, PhD. *People Skills: How to Assert Yourself, Listen to Others, And Resolve Conflicts.* New York: Simon & Schuster, 1986, p. 4-5, 32-39, 55, 59, 143.

Borba, Michele, EdD., "Hot Homework Tips for Parents: Ways to Minimize Our Nagging and Maximize Their Learning," posted on the Parenting Bookmark website, http://www.parentingbookmark.conm/pages/articleMB05.htm

CancerNet, "Helping a Child or Teenager Who is Grieving," posted on the American Cancer Society website, www.cancer.net/patient/coping/Grief-and-Bereavement/Helping-Grieving-Children

Carlson Johanna, "The Basic Needs of Every Child," posted on the Health Guidance website, http://www.healthguidance.org/entry/14969/1/The-Basic-Needs-of-Every-Child.html

Carpenter, Lisa, "6 Family Stories to Tell Your Grandchildren Again and Again," posted on the Huffington Post website, http://www.huffingtompost.com/2013/09/08/national-grandparents-day-2013_n_3873841.html

Chicago Tribune, "Grandparents Raising Grandchildren," http://.chicagotribune.com/classified/realestate/chi-primetime-grandparent-0226110

Coffey, Laura T., "10 Tips for Grandparents Raising Grandchildren: How to Avoid a Financial Shipwreck When Raising Your Children's Children," posted on the Today website, http://today/msnbc.com/od/16876875/ns/today-money/tips-grandparnets-raising-grand

Concept to Classroom, "Why Are Afterschool Programs Good for School-Age Children and Youth?", posted on the Concept to Classroom website, http://www.thirteen.org/edonline/concept2class/afterschool/index_sub3.html

Cornell University, "Role Changes/Transitions: Grandparents Raising Grandchildren," posted on the Cornell University website, www.cornellcares.org/pdf/handouts/rct_grandparents.pdf

CuteWriting, "Power of Short Sentences," posted on the CuteWriting blog, http://cutewriting.blogspot.com/2008/06/power-of-short-sentences.html

Dannison, Linda, PhD, CFLS and Smith, Andrea B., PhD, LSW, "Understanding Emotional Issues in Your Grandchildren's Lives," posted on the Family Information Services website, www.umich/edu/grs/forms/understanding-emotional-issues.pdf

Eisenberg, Richard, "Grandparents Raising Grandkids: Money Squeeze," posted on the Next Avenue website, http://www.nextavenue.org/grandparents-caring-for-grandkids-the-money-squeeze/

Euromed Info, "How Culture Influences Health Beliefs," posted on the Euromed Info website, http://www.euromedinfo.eu/how-culture-influences-health-believs.html/

Evitt, Marie Faust, "How to Teach Kids Perseverance and Goal-Setting," posted on the Parents Magazine website, http://www.parents.com/parenting/better-parenting/stle/how-to-teach-kids-perseverance-goal-setting/

Family Doctor Editorial Staff, "Oppositional Defiant Disorder," posted on the Family Doctor website, http://familydoctor.org/online/famdocen/home/common/mental/health/kids/953.html

Family Education, "Perfecting the Art of the Compliment," posted on the Family Education website, http://life.familyeducation. com/compliments/communication-skills/48978.html

Fay, Jim and Cline, Foster W., M.D., *Grandparenting with Love & Logic*. Golden, CO: The Love and Logic Press, Inc., 1994, p. 62, 134-135, 185

Ferrer-Chancy, Millie, Forthun, Larry F., and Falcone, Angela, "Grandparents Raising Grandchildren: Building Strong Families," posted on the University of Florida Extension website, http:// edis/ifas.ufl.edu

Ferrer-Chancy, Millie, Forthun, Larry F. Falcone, Angela and Pergola, Joe, "Grandparents Raising Grandchildren: Understanding Relationships," posted on the University of Florida Extension website, http://edis.ifas.ufl.edu.fv435

Frank, Christina, "The Need for Parenting Consistency," posted on the Parenting website, http://www.parenting.com/article/ the-need-for-consistency

Gaillard, Kathy, "More African American Parents are Raising Grandchildren," posted on the National Grandparents Raising Grandchildren Examiner website, http://www.examiner.com/ grandparents-raising-grandchildren-in-national/more-african-am

Gilbert, Elizabeth, "Let's Talk About Those Happiness Jars, Shall We?" posted on Elizabeth Gilbert's website, http://www. elizabethgilbert.com/lets-talk-about-those-happiness-jars-shall-we-dear-lovelies-about-a-y/

Goleman, Daniel, *Emotional Intelligence: Why it Can Matter More Than IQ*. New York: Bantam Books, 1997, p. 87.

Goyer, Amy, "More Grandparents Raising Grandkids: New Census Data Shows an Increase in Children Being Raised by Extended Family," posted on the AARP website, http://www.aarp.org/relationships/grandparenting/info-12-2010/more_grandparents_raising

Grandparents Weekly, "Tax Tips for Grandparents Raising Grandchildren," posted on the Grandparents Weekly website, http://www.parentingweekly.com/grandparents/taxtips.htm

Grief Speaks, "Teen Grief in School," posted on the Grief Speaks website, http://www.griefspeaks.com/id36.html

Grohol, John M., PsyD, "5 Secrets to a Successful Long-Term Relationship or Marriage," posted on the PsychCentral website, http://psychcentra.com/lib/2007/5-secrets-to-a-successful-long-term-relationship-or-marria

Grollman, Earl A., *Straight Talk About Death for Teenagers: How to Cope with Losing Someone You Love*. Boston: Beacon Press, 1993, p. 33.

Horsley, Dr. Heidi and Horsley, Dr. Gloria, *Teen Grief Relief: Parenting with Understanding, Support and Guidance*. Highland City, FL: Rainbow Books, 2007, p. xix, xx, 49.

Jacobs, Barry J., "4 Tips for Better Sleep While Caregiving," posted on the AARP website, http://www.aarp.org/home-family/home-family-experts/caregiving-advice-barry-jacobs.html

Kasdin, Karin, "Grandparents Raising Grandchildren: 'Twice the Stress of Average Parents,'" posted on the Huffington Post website, http://www.huffingtonpost.com/karin-kasdin/when-grandparents-raise-grandchidren_b_1267476.html

Kenison, Katrina, *The Gift of an Ordinary Day: A Mother's Memoir.* New York: Grand Central Publishing, 2009, p. 253-255.

Kids Health, "Bereavement Reactions by Age Group," posted on the Kids Health website, http://kidshealth.org.nz/bereavement-reactions-age-group

Kids Health, "Household Safety Checklists," posted on the Kids Health website, http://kidshealth.org/en/parents/household-checklist-kitchen.html

Kraft, Sheryl, "8 Surprising Sleep Stealers," posted on the American Grandparents Association website, www.grandparents.com/health-and-wellbeing-health/why-cant-i-sleep

Laden, Meredith, "Understanding the Five Essentials Children Need from Parents," posted on the Bright Hub website, http://www.brighthub/com/parenting/grade-school/articles/62175.aspx

Lilly (no last name), "Caring Conversations: Caregiving Loneliness During the Holidays," posted on the CareGiving website, http://www.caregiving.com/2016/12/caregiver-loneliness-holidays/

Livestrong, "List of Life Skills Children Should Have," posted on the Livestrong website, http://www.livestrong.com/articles/125579-list-of-life-skills-children-should/

Mayo Clinic Staff, "Caregiver Depression: Prevention Counts," posted on the Mayo Clinic website, http://www.mayoclinic.org/healthy-lifestyle/caregivers/in-depth/caregiver-depressio/art20047051

Mayo Clinic Staff, "Sleep Deprivation: Not a Normal Part of Aging," "Mayo Clinic Health Letter," September 2011, p. 6.

Meuser, Thomas M., PhD and Marwit, Samuel J., PhD, "MM Caregiver Grief Inventory-Short Form," alzheimer.wustl.edu/About_Us/PDFs/MM-CGI-50 Full Version.pdf

Moffatt, Bettyclare, *Soulwork: Clearing the Mind, Opening the Heart, Replenishing the Spirit*. Berkeley, CA: Wildcat Canyon Press, 1994, p. 36.

Morin, Amanda, "Setting Back-to-School Goals," posted on The Spruce website, https://thespruce.com/setting-tack-to-school-goals-2086626

Muhammad, Charlene, "Millions are Raising Their Grandkids in Poverty," posted on the American Media website, http://newamericanmedia.org/2011/03/millions-are-raising-their-grandkids-in-poverty.php

Myers, Seth, PsyD, "How Financial Problems & Stress Cause Divorce," posted on the Psychology Today website, https://www.psychologytoday.com/blog/insight-is-2020/201212/how-financial-problems-stress-cause-divorce

Noel, Brook and Blair, Pamela D., PhD., *I Wasn't Ready to Say Goodbye: Surviving, Coping & Healing After the Sudden Death of a Loved One*. Milwaukee, WI: Champion Press, Ltd., 2000, p. 84-89.

Ohio State University, "Grandparents as Parents Again," posted on the Ohio State University Extension website, http://ohioline.osu.edu/ss-fact/0157.html

Original Play, "The Importance of Original Play in Human Development," posted on the Original Play website, http://www.originalplay.com/develop.htm

Pichardt, Carl, PhD., "Surviving Your Child's Adolescence," posted on the Psychology Today website, http://www.psychologytoday.

com/blog/surviving-your-child-adolescense/101003/ adolescense

Picchi, Aimee, "For 'Grandfamilies,' Raising Grandkids can Mean Going Broke," posted on the MoneyWatch website, http://www. cbsnews.com/news/raising-grandkids-and-going-broke/

Poe, Leonora M., "Connecting the Bridges: Grandparenting Children," posted on the University of Wisconsin website, http:// parenthood.ibrary.wisc.edu?poe/poe.html

Pond, Natalie and Hense, Hanne, "Revising for Clarity," posted on The Center for Writing and Speaking blog, https:// whitmanwriting.wordpress.com/2014/04/04/revising-for-clarity/

Population Reference Bureau, "The Health and Well-Being of Grandparents Caring for Grandchildren", www.prb.org/pdf11/ TodaysResearchAging23.pdf

Ransford, Marc, "Grandparents More Loving, Strict When Raising Youngsters," posted on the Ball State University website, http:// www.bsu.edu/news/article/0.1370.-1019-272.00.html

Reynolds, Glenda Phillips, Wright, James V., and Beale, Betty, "The Roles of Grandparents in Educating Today's Children," posted on the Journal of Instructional Psychology website, www. thefreelibrary.com

Ross, Maisie, Forthun, Larry F., Ferrer-Chancy, Millie and Falcone, Angela, "Grandparents Raising Grandchildren: Health Care Assistance," posted on the University of Florida website, http:// edis.ifas.ufl.edu/pdffiles/FY/FY112300.pdf

Salek, Elyse C., Med and Ginsburg, Kenneth R., MD, MS Ed, FAAP,

"How Children Understand Death & What You Should Say," posted on the Healthy Children website, https://www. healthychildren.org/English/healthy-living/emotional-wellness/Building-Resilience/Pages/How-Children-Understand-Death-What-You-Should-Say

Seashore, Charles N., PhD, "Developing and Using Personal Support Systems," www.socialwork.ou.edu/Wesites/socialwork /images/MSW/resources/

SleepDisordersGuide, "Sleep Apnea Statistics," posted on the SleepDisordersGuide website, http://www.sleepdisordersguide. com/articles/skeeo-disorders/

Smith, Kurt, PsyD, LMFT, LPCC, AFC, "Silence: The Secret Communication Tool," posted on the PsychCentral website, https://psychcentral.com/sss/06/silence-the-secret-communication-tool

State of Wisconsin, "Constructive Criticism: Giving It . . . and Receiving It!" posted on the Wisconsin Toolbox Talk website, www.dwd.wisconsin.gov/apparenticeship/pdf/TBT01_ConstructiveCriticism.pdf

Stitch, Sally, "8 Activities Kids Love to Do with Grandparents," posted on the American Grandparents Association website, http://www.grandprents.com/grandkids/activities-games-and-crafts/things-do-grandkids

Stosney, Steve, PhD, "Pain and Suffering," posted on the Psychology Today website, https://psychologytoday.com/blog/ anger-in-the-age-entitlement/201104/pain-and-suffering

Stosney, Steven, PhD, "The Meaning of Emotional Pain," posted on the Psychology Today website, https://www.psychologytoday.com/blog/anter-in-the-age-entitlement/201107/the-meaning-emotional-pain

Tannen, Deborah, PhD., *That's Not What I Meant! How Conversational Style Makes or Breaks Relationships*. New York: Ballantine Books, 1996, p. 39, 122, 180.

Tatelbaum, Judy, *The Courage to Grieve: Creative Living, Recovery & Growth Through Grief*. New York: Harper & Row, Publishers, Inc., 1980, p. 10, 31, 139.

Teach Kids How, "How to Give and Receive a Compliment," posted on the Teach Kids How website, http://www.teachkidshow.com/how-to-give-and-receive-a-compliment

Toastmasters International, "Your Speaking Voice," posted on the Toastmasters International website, www.toastmasters.org/-/media/B7D5C3FC34343589BCBF5DBF521132.ashx

The Town Talk, "Child's Play: Importance of Play Time for Children Neglected, Advocates Say," posted on The Town Talk website, http://www.thetowntalk.com/article/20110823/LIFESTYLE/10823036/Child-s-Play-Impor

University of Michigan, "Bad Habits/Annoying Behavior," posted on the University of Michigan Health System website, http://www.med/umich.edu/yourchild/optics/badhabit.html

US Government, Department of Education, "Homework Tips for Parents," posted on the ED.gov website, http://www.2.ed.gov/print/parents/academic/involve/homework/part.html

US Government, Food and Drug Administration, "Changes to the Nutrition Facts Label," posted on the FDA website, https://www.fda.gov/Food/GuidanceRegulation/Guidance DocmentsRegulatoryInformation/LabeligNutrition/ucm385663. htm

Valeo, Tom, "Strategies for Happiness: 7 Steps to Becoming a Happy Person," posted on the webMD website, http://www. webmd.com/balance/guide/choosing-to-be-happy

Whitbourne, Susan Krauss, PhD, "The Ultimate Guide to Body Language," posted on the Psychology Today website, https:// www.psychologytoday.com/blog/fulfillment-any-age-201206/ the-ultimate-guide-to-body-language

Whitley, Deborah M., PhD, Kelly, Susan J., PhD, "Grandparents Raising Grandchildren: A Call to Action," posted on the Early Childhood Learning & Knowledge Center website, http:// eclkc.ohs.acf.hhs.gov/hslc/tta-system/family/Family%20 and20%Community%20Par

Wiltz, Teresa, "How Drug Addiction Led to More Grandparents Raising Their Grandchildren," posted on the PBS Newshour web-site, http://www.pbs.org/newshor.rundown/drug-addiction-led -grandparents-raising-grandchildren/

Wolfelt, Alan D., PhD., *Healing Your Grieving Heart for Teens: 100 Practical Ideas.* Fort Collins, CO: Companion Press, 2001, entire book.

Zucker, Bonnie, Dr., "Parents are Asking: Why is a Consistent Routine Important?" posted on the Parents Ask website, http://www.parentsask.com/articles/parents-are-asking-why-consistent-routine-important

About the Author

Harriet Hodgson, BS, MA, has been a writer for thirty-eight years. She is the author of thirty-six books and thousands of print and online articles. She is a member of the Association of Health Care Journalists, the Minnesota Coalition for Death Education and Support, and the Grief Coalition of Southeastern

Photo courtesy of Elizabeth Nida Obert, Senior Photographer, Post-Bulletin newspaper, Rochester, MN.

Minnesota. Hodgson is a contributing writer for The Caregiver Space website, Open to Hope Foundation website, and The Grief Toolbox website.

She has appeared on more than 185 radio talk shows, including CBS Radio, and dozens of television stations, including CNN. Hodgson has also been a guest on many BlogTalkRadio programs. A popular speaker, she has given presentations at public health, Alzheimer's, bereavement, and caregiving conferences.

Hodgson's work is cited in *Who's Who of American Women*, *World Who's Who of Women*, *Contemporary Authors*, and other directories. She lives in Rochester, Minnesota, with her husband, John. Please visit www.harriethodgson.com for more information about this busy wife, grandmother, caregiver, and author.

Index

A
abuse, 10, 13, 42, 63
acceptance, 114, 126
active listening, 89-90
Acquired Immune Deficiency Syndrome (AIDS), 9, 45
addiction, 5, 9, 11, 20
adjustment, 12, 27, 42
after school activities and programs, 105-106
aggressive behaviors, 13
ambivalence, 12
anger, 138
   grandchild's, 55, 94
   grandparent's, 12, 114, 115
   marital, 28
   outbursts, 32
anxiety, 13, 36, 138
   grandchild's, 53-54
art, 119-120
Attention Deficit Disorder (ADD), 42

B
barriers, 100-101
basic needs
   mental, 62-63
   physical, 62, 63, 66

H

I

J

K

S

T

V

W